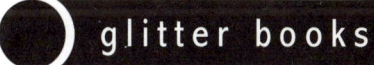

glitter books

TICKET TO RIDE
Alasdair Ferguson & Alf Bicknell
ISBN 1 902588 01 0
Published By
THE GLITTERBOOKS OF LONDON
Copyright © Alasdair Ferguson, Alf Bicknell
& Glitter Books 1999

Alf, good old Alf, who chauffered us around and helped out
as a Roadie during the days of Beatlemania. Alf was special
though. Not only did he accompany us through an important
period in our career, but he always had a great sense of humour
and could handle the teasing that inevitably came with the job.
Not everyone you meet is loyal, not everybody is someone you can
trust, and not everyone is a likeable person, but Alf scored easily
on all three points.

He came with us through the craziness, the emotion, the fun and
the nonsense, and I was always glad to have had him on our side.

Alf Bicknell was originally hired to be the Beatles chauffeur in 1964 and although he drove us everywhere for the following few years -- he did so much more than that. Along with Neil Aspinall and Mal Evans, Alf Bicknell lived moment to moment with the Beatles through those years sharing every moment from dawn to dusk (sometimes dawn to dawn) in cars, planes, trains, hotels, concert halls -- every minute of those tours -- Alf was present.

Alf was a friend-protector-bodyguard and confidant, serving us through the fun and also the tough times.

During those exciting but hectic years it was so important to John, Paul, Ringo and myself to have help from people we knew we could trust. To not have to worry about whether the right arrangements were being made for our travel and security or for maybe just a good pot of tea! Trust maybe is just a word we have heard around a wide-angled curve, but we all have experienced trust misplaced over the last 25 years and I can tell you all it is pretty ugly. Alf, along with Neil and Mal, was priceless. Their contribution to the "Fabness" of us four was immeasurable, yet through the years that followed -- having had plenty of opportunities to "sell" their "true story" - the real true story is that they were our uncorruptible friends and we all know that no amount of money can buy true friendship.

Anybody who was beaten up by Imelda Marcos' bully squad is a friend of mine! Even back in Manila in 1965 (?) we had a gut feeling that the Marcos' were vile. The Beatles always had good taste!

I hope you (the reader) enjoy "The Beatles Chauffeur" as much as we did, and incidently Alf -- I'm still in Bob Dylan's wardrobe.

                    With love,

                    George Harrison.

Dear Alf – as promised :-   21 . 12 . 94.

Alf Bicknell was a rare breed of Chauffeur.
He was thrown into the madness and mayhem
of that phenomena Beatlemania
He did virtually everything during that time
for John + the boys except bathing them and
putting them to bed!
To have Survived Such an experience as that of
the 60's. The ultimate criteria was to have a
very good sense of the ridiculous and above
all else, a temperament of a saint to cope.
Alf had all those qualities and more.
We had memorable times together and as
friends, still, we who are here to tell the tale
the way it was.
                              Cynthia Lennon.

P.S. Hope it's OK for you Alf good luck with the book.

CONTENTS

PICTURE DETAILS

Author's Acknowledgements

Special thanks to Alasdair Ferguson for the long hours and work into bringing my story to life.
Thanks to Donna Mosessian for the great photo she took of Cynthia Lennon, and my love to her – a special friend.

Jack Edwards, who has worked tirelessly to help me tell my story – my love to him.
To Beatles fans around the world: enjoy – love from me to you.

Jeff Jones, who took a special photo of Paul and I.

Special thanks and love to my family, who have put up with my ups and downs trying to put this piece of social history together.

To John, Paul, George and Ringo – thank you for being great passengers; my love, loyalty and friendship always.

Patti Selke, my dear friend – through all her pain and suffering, she has been there for me; God bless her.

And to all those who are no longer with us – they will always be in our hearts and prayers.

—Love, Alf.

Ticket To Ride

The Ultimate Beatles Tour Diary!

Alasdair Ferguson & Alf Bicknell

Alf and Cynthia Lennon, 1991 (© Donna Mosessian).

FOREWORD

IN mid-December 1997, I was working as a sub-editor at the *Scottish Daily Express* in Glasgow, when a call came through from a press officer at a small video company.

As a sideline to my work editing the copy of staff and contributors at the *Express*, I would do the occasional star interview. These were usually with minor celebrities, who were trying to get some newspaper space to promote their new book or video. That particular call, if I remember correctly, was from the press office dealing with *Vogue* from The Gladiators, who had just released a new exercise video.

Apparently *Vogue* was pleased with the piece and the PR office was wondering if there were any other of their clients I would like to chat to. As they listed the publicity-hungry celebs, only one momentarily caught my attention. It was a name I'd never heard before but his CV did sound intriguing.

Apparently Alf Bicknell had spent three years as chauffeur to The Beatles.

Still not entirely convinced by the pitch – I'd learned people will do anything to plug their products – I agreed to a phone interview with Alf, who was releasing a video based on his experiences with the Fab Four. Several days later, I called him up and began the interview.

I can't remember exactly when it struck me – his meeting with Elvis, battling Phillipinos, who were furious at what they saw as a snub by The Beatles to their premier Imelda Marcos, or his sex and drugs encounter with Bob Dylan – but I soon realised this was the most extra-ordinary man I had ever interviewed.

I told the *Express* boss this particular story merited more than the double page spread usually allotted for such pieces.

Alf Bicknell's story was eventually told over three days around New Year – but I had grander ideas.

This was a tale that needed telling in full, but I had realised in my dealings with Alf that he was desperately publicity-shy.

The tabloids had already tried to get him

to spill the beans on the Beatles. Six-figure sums had been offered for the gory details of George, John, Paul and Ringo. But to no avail.

Alf was adamant he wouldn't sully the memory of his time in the midst of Beatlemania with a tacky tabloid front page splash.

His mistrust of the media was palpable.

None the less I sent him cuttings of the three features in *The Express* and left him my home phone number and asked him to call me with his verdict.

On New Year's Eve I was in the bath when the call came. As I sat shivering and dripping in the hallway, Alf bellowed down the phone: "You've captured the spirit perfectly."

He was pleased, so I didn't hesitate.

"Listen, I think this would make a great book. If I can find a publisher will you let me tell the story?"

He thought for a moment and then agreed.

Within about three days, bearing in mind I had never written a book before, I had several offers from publishers and had secured a deal within a week.

Many phone calls later, hours of tape and a few visits to Alf's home in Banbury, Oxfordshire, and I had the raw materials for the book.

So here it is.

Those looking for pinpoint accuracy, dates, times, set-lists and so on, may be disappointed. I feel that has been done many times before by people with an encyclopaedic knowledge of The Beatles' history.

Instead, I like to think this book comes from a different angle. It witnesses famous events such as the aforementioned meeting of Elvis and the Beatles, or their reaction when the Ku Klux Klan vowed to have them assassinated, from a new perspective – Alf's.

As he has said himself on many occasions, he liked to adopt an "out-of-camera" approach with the band. In the background, almost unseen but always there in case he was needed.

Above all, though, I hope I have done justice to the memories he chose to share with me of his three magical years as chauffeur, bodyguard, confidante and friend of The Beatles.

PROLOGUE
Birmingham NEC, January 8 1990

PAUL McCartney was midway through an energetic set. Solo songs, tracks from his days with Wings and, of course, Beatles standards had kept the audience, which ranged from teenagers right up to die-hard Fab Four fans, happy. Then came an impromptu moment in an otherwise tightly-rehearsed show, where even the most spontaneous-seeming ad-lib had been carefully thought out. McCartney looked out into the sea of faces and announced he wanted to dedicate the next track to an old and dear friend. The other band members stared at each other mystified. "Alf, this is for you," said Paul. "I've never forgotten."

Way back in the giant amphitheatre, the eyes of the man the rock legend had made the dedication to, began to well up with tears.

As the opening chords of "The Long And Winding Road" began to echo round the hall, Alf Bicknell's mind flooded with golden memories, of his three precious years as an employee and close friend of The Beatles.

It was nearly 26 years ago...

CHAPTER ONE

October, 1964; Devonshire Close,
London

THERE was a knock at the door of the flat in Devonshire Close. Jean Bicknell opened the door to an unfamiliar face. A hand was proffered to her by way of introduction. "Hello, I'm from NEMS Enterprises," said the stranger. Before Jean could begin to work out the mysterious acronym – North End Music Stores, Brian Epstein's London Offices – the unfamiliar but polite visitor, continued: "Is Alf Bicknell in?" Jean, still somewhat perplexed by the man on her doorstep, called her husband, who arrived shortly to be greeted by the stranger.

"Hi, we haven't met before – but I can put some work your way, if you're interested," the man offered.

Alf, who had been chauffeuring for seven years but had just left his last firm, and was, as they say "resting between appointments", was curious.

"I'm certainly looking for something," he enquired cautiously.

The visitor shot back: "How would you feel about a rock band?"

Alf, who had chauffeured the likes of David Niven, Sophia Loren and Peter Cushing, had had little experience of ferrying pop stars about, but he was interested and up for the challenge.

"Possibly," he said, "Who is it?"

The stranger paused, looked briefly from side to side, before continuing: "It's The Beatles."

Alf's stomach suddenly started to churn. He was speechless for a moment.

His potential future employer enquired: "You *have* heard of them?"

Alf attempted to hide his nervousness. He had, throughout his time as a chauffeur to the stars, prided himself on being relaxed around them. For the periods they spent in the back of his limo, he was keen that they shouldn't feel he was in any way overawed or intimidated by them.

But – THE BEATLES!

Already they had a string of chart-topping singles under their belts, such as "Please Please Me", "She Loves You" and "I Want To Hold Your Hand".

On a daily basis, news reports in papers and on TV would breathlessly tell of the growing phenomenon that was Beatlemania.

From every magazine rack, the faces of the four moptops from Liverpool would smile impishly on the covers of glossy monthlies.

Love them, or loathe them, The Beatles were quite simply impossible to ignore.

Alf came back to his senses and stammered: "Of course, yes, I've heard of them. I'm interested."

The stranger replied coolly: "Good, I'll let them know and we'll set up a meeting."

Then, he was gone.

The bewildered chauffeur closed the door, still somewhat shaken, and went back inside.

Jean asked what was going on but her husband was lost in a world of his own as he plumped himself down in his armchair, still wondering if he had dreamt the encounter.

Was the whole thing a wind-up? I mean, working for The Beatles? What's the catch? he thought to himself.

And why had he been plucked from comparative obscurity for the task of ferrying around The Fab Four, rapidly and almost effortlessly asserting themselves as the most important creative musical force in the Twentieth Century.

Alf decided to put the matter from his mind, and life at Devonshire Close returned to normal... but not for much longer.

He had several agonising days to wait for the next piece in the jigsaw to fall into place.

As promised, the call duly came from the NEMS representative.

A meeting was set up for Alf to meet with John, Paul, George and Ringo at Brian Epstein's office in King Williams' Mews in the city.

Several days later, a decidedly edgy and nervous Alf turned up at the appointed time and knocked on the door of the NEMS premises.

Almost immediately the door swung

open, a friendly face beamed out and Alf was shaking the hand of Epstein's assistant, Lonnie Trimball.

"I've been expecting you. Come in," said Lonnie graciously.

He took Alf through to a small office and sat him down at a table.

Lonnie was the man who ensured all Epstein's visitors were kept happy, while they waited for the arrival of The Beatles boss.

He quickly produced a bottle of Scotch, a bottle of coke and some cigarettes, and urged the driver to help himself.

Alf, still incredibly nervous about meeting the Fab Four, sought comfort in the hospitality afforded him and began making serious inroads into the whisky.

Two hours later, Lonnie returned to say he didn't think the great meeting was going to take place.

At this stage, this was probably a good thing for Alf.

A bellyful of whisky coupled with his nerves would have made him appear a less than suitable candidate for chauffeur to the four brightest minds in the pop world.

He swayed as he got up and staggered to the door.

Lonnie bundled him into a cab and that was the end of that, save for the pounding hangover the next day, only made worse by a feeling he had blown his chances of entering the inner sanctum of The Beatles.

Several days later he received a further summons, however.

Alf was in his flat, when he got the somewhat frantic phone call.

"Hello, this is Alistair Taylor," said Brian Epstein's assistant.

"Can you get hold of a limousine – an Austin Princess?"

Alf thought for a moment, then said: "Give me a few minutes."

He quickly called his old hire firm Empress Cars and asked: "Any chance you could give me a loan of an Austin Princess?"

His old boss replied: "Well, maybe, what's it for?"

Alf thought for a second and then decided to keep it a bit vague: "Well, it's driving a rock band about. These, erm, four guys."

The voice on the end of the line paused then replied: "Yeah, we can do that – we'll have it ready in a few hours or so. You can pick it up then."

Alf quickly phoned Alistair Taylor back, and confirmed he'd located a suitable vehicle: "Yeah, I've got one – I can pick it up in a few hours or so."

Taylor responded: "OK, good, write this down, then."

He gave the driver an address in South West London and added: "But it needs to be quicker than a few hours – they'll be ready shortly."

Alf responded uncertainly: "Look, I'll do my best."

He immediately phoned Empress back and pleaded: "Look, I need this right away."

His former boss replied somewhat disgruntledly: "Well, come and get it. I suppose it's OK as it is. We were going to clean it up for you."

Alf jumped in a cab and headed over to Kensington to pick up the Princess.

Then he drove round to Earls Court to meet with his future employers.

The venue was a photographic studio, where Bob Freeman – who did many of The Beatles photos – was doing a shoot with them.

Freeman's work included the classic shadow-faced Fab Four cover shot for the *With The Beatles* album.

Alf sat outside the building in the Princess waiting for the band. Suddenly the studio door opened. Four figures flew towards the Austin Princess, its back door was flung open and there they were:– one – two – three – The Fab Four – they were in the back of the car.

A fifth figure raced round to the front and climbed into the passenger's seat next to Alf.

The seal had been broken. Alf was now in the employ of John, Paul, George and Ringo.

His life would never be the same again.

CHAPTER TWO
King Williams Mews, London

ALF Bicknell's first mission as chauffeur to the Fab Four was, to say the least, something of a disaster. After picking the boys up from the photo shoot, he began the drive to King Williams Mews, as instructed by Beatles tour manager Neil Aspinall, who sat next to him in the passenger's seat. Still a complete virgin to the hysterical monster that was Beatlemania, the driver was completely unprepared for what was to follow over the next few minutes – and indeed, the next few years.

"I became aware of what I can only describe as a buzz," recalls Alf.

He's not referring to some kind of metaphorical air of importance surrounding the band. This was the actual "sound" of Beatlemania, which followed the group everywhere.

"And this buzz gradually became louder

and more intense and soon there were what seemed like millions of teenage screams filling the air."

As the Austin Princess pulled up to each set of traffic lights, teenage girls began to gather round the car, pursuing it from junction to junction.

Their ear-splitting screams seemed to act as a sonic signal to other crazed fans.

None of Alf Bicknell's seven years of chauffeuring had prepared him for what Paul McCartney dubbed "the eye of the hurricane".

As the crowds began to gather round the car, Alf began to panic.

Suddenly he jammed his foot on the brakes and the Austin Princess screeched to an unscheduled emergency stop, sending the Fab Four flying.

George Harrison came off worst.

The youngest Beatle had cracked his head off the seat in front.

A nervous glance in the rear-view mirror confirmed the driver's worst fears – Harrison was not a happy camper.

"He looked extremely angry. I remember

I thought to myself, *Well, that's that, the briefest job I've ever had,*" laughs Alf.

He attempted to apologise, as a red-faced Harrison stroked his aching brow.

Suddenly, Alf discovered he had an ally sitting right next to him.

Neil immediately took control of the tense situation, insisting the chauffeur had had no other course of action.

The slightly bruised guitarist nodded reluctantly and the matter was forgotten.

Alf started the engine and the journey continued, mercifully without further incident.

It was clear that the driver's fears that he had just lost probably the most sought-after job in chauffeuring were to be proved wrong.

And all thanks to Neil.

But Alf still had everything to prove loyalty-wise to the band, if he was to be allowed into the close-knit Beatles inner sanctum, which comprised of the band, roadie Mal Evans, manager Brian Epstein, and tour manager Neil Aspinall.

Indeed, the very reason Alf had been offered the job in the first place had been because of an appalling breach of loyalty by his predecessor.

The previous driver had dropped the band off at Heathrow Airport, where they flew off for a tour of the States.

He then drove into London's Fleet Street, parked the limousine and headed up to a Sunday newspaper, where he sold his story for a hefty sum.

Not surprisingly he was given his marching orders and The Beatles' suspicion of newcomers was intensified.

"It was difficult for me to say, 'Listen, guys, trust me' – because of what the previous guy had done," Alf says now.

He decided there were two ways to try a win the trust and respect of his employers. He could declare his honest intentions from the start and reason that one bad chauffeur shouldn't cast a shadow over all drivers.

Or he could let his actions speak for themselves and prove his loyalty.

He decided on the latter option and kept his head down over the next few months.

When he took the chauffeuring job, the

group were in the middle of their British tour, which started on October 9 at the Gaumont Cinema in Bradford and ended at Bristol's Colston Hall on November 10.

This was the band's only British tour of 1964 and was, therefore, eagerly awaited by their loyal and fervent fans. Packed houses were treated to a set of Fab Four classics, including "Twist And Shout", "Can't Buy Me Love", "Hard Day's Night" and "Long Tall Sally".

Despite the gruelling work schedule – The Beatles performed two shows per date on the tour – the boys were reluctant to stay in any of the cities if driving back to London was an option.

Alf quickly became part of the touring machine.

The chauffeur, obviously the "new boy" in the Fab Four camp, took a while to learn the ropes.

He would liaise carefully with Neil Aspinall to find out about dates and pick-up points to take his charges through the screaming hordes to the "various Gaumonts, Odeons and so on, up and down the country".

"Neil would let me know where we were headed each day. Shepherd's Bush, Walthamstow – wherever."

This almost daily ritual continued from the day that Alf joined them up until mid-November, as they laboriously made their way through the UK tour.

"Up until Christmas time, we were running up and down the country to different venues day after day – constant touring.

"Ringo and Brian each had flats at King Williams Mews, so that became the pick-up point. There was an underground car park and I'd drive the Austin Princess in there," reveals Alf.

"John and Paul would wander in and George would arrive in his mini. Ringo would come down from his apartment and we'd all head off in the Austin Princess."

The band had engagements all over England but, as was almost always the case, they were keen on returning to London each night.

"They hardly stayed anywhere. We'd do Brighton, then come back again. Bournemouth, back again, Southampton, back again,

Birmingham, back again. This was when it began to get really tough for me," sighs Alf.

"We would only stay in hotels if we travelled much further afield. Manchester, Gateshead and so on.

"It was exhausting. I remember waking some mornings and being filled with trepidation. Filled with the feeling that I couldn't do it, that I couldn't go on at this pace," he sighs. Meanwhile, the band were becoming bigger and bigger.

Alf's exhaustion, coupled with his fears that his four famous passengers would come to harm while in his care, began to take its toll.

"I was extremely nervous. But usually once I got into the car it was fine – although the madness was never far away. We'd be surrounded by screaming fans – some on foot, some on motorbikes, or some in cars. They'd jump all over the car writing their names in lipstick and so on."

The famous Liverpudlians were used to this extreme behaviour – their wit carried them through.

"It was an outlet for them, obviously.

This wonderful Liverpool banter would carry on regardless of the mayhem which was going on outside the car. But it was also an outlet for me in a way, and kept my spirits up," Alf recalls.

"I'd join in occasionally. I remember I'd wind them up just before the charts came out, if they'd released a single.

"I'd say, 'You know, I don't think you'll be number one this time,' looking round at them, sat in the back of the car. Of course, they always were."

Occasionally the routine would get even more hectic, with the band squeezing more than one engagement into one day, meaning a great deal more travelling for their chauffeur.

November 14 saw them interrupt the tour to record several songs at a television studio, then later, the night ended with John and Ringo heading out to a club.

Alf was needed from the early hours right through till the middle of the next morning.

"I had to pick them up one by one. That day I remember I had to struggle to get John out of bed. He was still asleep when I arrived at his house," recalls Alf.

"By that stage I knew them well enough to fool around with them, and John was always the one who made me laugh the most. I had to drag the covers off him so he would get up.

"I made him a cup of tea and we headed off to collect the others. Finally I managed to deliver all of them to the TV studios at Teddington, where they were doing a recording for *Thank Your Lucky Stars*."

John, Paul, George and Ringo looked bored and restless as they waited for what seemed like an eternity before the cameras rolled.

"As ever, when it was their turn to perform, they sprang into life, giving it their all as they played tracks like 'I Feel Fine' and 'I'm A Loser'.

"That night I took Ringo and John to the Flamingo Club, after dropping Paul and George off at their homes. As usual a bunch of pop stars and actors were at the club, where Georgie Fame and the Blue Flames were playing.

"The boys chatted and drank into the wee small hours and I waited patiently to take them home. I'd been with the band less than a month now, but I must admit that even by then I was beginning to find the long hours a bit of a strain."

In December, The Beatles took up a residency at London's Hammersmith Odeon for a series of shows.

"Leading up to the Christmas concerts, they were doing rehearsals for the Hammersmith gigs. The rehearsals and the actual concerts went on for about three or four weeks in all. I'd pick them up every day and run them to the Odeon and return for them at night."

The previous year's festive gigs had been a great success, so 1964's "Another Beatles Christmas Show" was eagerly anticipated.

By this stage, the previous disloyal chauffeur was a distant memory, and Alf had been accepted into the fold.

Together with Neil Aspinall and guitar roadie Mal Evans he formed a protective trio, which accompanied the group wherever they went.

Backstage at the Christmas shows, as Alf kept a watchful eye on his precious charges, he realised that despite their global domination in record sales, there were no pretensions about The Beatles.

"One of the first things I observed was, despite the fact they were performing every night, all four of the boys were gracious to everyone. Bands like Sound Incorporated or The Yardbirds – who were support acts – would pop into the dressing room.

"Despite the fact they were becoming hugely famous – unprecedently so – it didn't seem to affect them – they were great to everyone.

"I remember Jimmy Saville, who was one of the hosts of the show, had a dressing room above the band. He was always trying to get them to work out on his weights – he wanted them to get fit, I think."

The actual concerts were a strange mix of Beatles' music – standards like "Twist And Shout" and "Long Tall Sally" – and various rather juvenile comedy sketches.

However, subtlety was a not particularly important concern.

The entire festive season was performed in front of the usual constantly screaming hordes.

The shows would end with the legendary, "The Beatles have now left the building", and at that, Alf would be in control. The evening would usually finish with the driver taking the boys along to a nightclub.

He'd park the Princess and head up with the famous foursome, keeping a watchful but discreet eye on his precious charges.

"We'd go to all the top night spots. The Ad Lib club or some of the trendy joints in Duke Street. Various places," recalls Alf.

"Always I'd be on coke – the bottled variety. I obviously had to have a very strict regime, so I would be ready to ferry the group and their friends wherever they wanted to go.

"The Ad Lib club, which was just off Leicester Square, was probably the first place I started taking them after the Christmas shows."

Club-owners would be delighted they had the world's top pop band in their venue.

The entourage would sweep in, and the best table in the house would soon be ready and waiting for them.

"I don't know if they knew in advance – the club proprietors. But we would turn up and they would be whisked in without question. They were The Beatles and that was that."

But despite their global domination, all four Beatles, as ever, kept their feet firmly on the ground. "That's what always struck me. Whenever they popped out, they were great. So easy-going and willing to chat to fans, other celebrities, whoever wanted a natter.

"When we settled down in a club they would rarely sit around together, they'd be off chatting to folk, mingling with people at other tables.

"Often Patti would come in and sit with George, or Cyn would join John for a drink, or Ringo would be with Maureen and in those days, of course, Paul would be with Jane Asher."

Along with Joe Public, the Fab Four were, not surprisingly, surrounded by the foremost celebrities of the time.

"Jagger, the rest of the Stones, Long John Baldry, The Animals, Eric Clapton – everybody. There were so many – too numerous for me to remember.

"But my eyes were, as ever, watching over John, Paul, George and Ringo."

Amazingly, during this potentially vulnerable situation for the band, exposed to the public as they let their moptops down, there was never any trouble.

"That was the nice thing, there was never any hassle. I remember it was usually late at night when we'd descend on these clubs.

"I would try to be out of 'camera shot', as I called it. Just to be present to fulfil what was needed of me."

Alf's chauffeuring position became a regular taxi-ing service. Not just for the band, but also for the various celebs that hung around the Fab Four.

George, John, or someone would pipe up to whomever they had finished speaking to: "Oh, are you going? Alf will drop you off."

And the driver would happily oblige.

"I'd take all these stars – Sandie Shaw, or whoever – back to their homes or wherever they wanted to go."

"They'd jump into the back of The Princess, often a bit drunk, and I'd drive off. Then it was back to the club to see if anyone else wanted a lift."

The driver's sleeping hours were, at first, hard to grow used to. "I'd be up until the wee small hours dropping various celebrities off and, of course, the band.

"Then back to my flat, trying not to wake Jean, for a few hours kip.

"Then I'd be up a short while later – sometimes just three or four hours – preparing to take the boys to, at that time, the Hammersmith Odeon."

But on the whole, it was relatively straightforward.

"This was thankfully an easy time for me. It was constant. To the Hammersmith, wait till the show was over, off to a club or straight back to King Williams Mews.

"George, Paul and John would jump into their various cars and Ringo would head off to his apartment in the building there."

But the long unsociable hours were taking their toll on family life.

"I saw so little of Jean, or Mark our son, in those days," he sighs.

The Beatles were never privy – very deliberately on Alf's part – to the troubles –

tragedies, even, taking place in his private life.

"I didn't share my problems. For example, there was a time when Jean and myself were staying at Devonshire Close, shortly after I started with The Beatles. Jean was pregnant."

One terrible Sunday morning, things were to go horribly wrong.

"Jean was very distressed. She thought she was having a miscarriage, which ultimately it turned out to be.

"We were right in the heart of London – a stone's throw from Harley Street.

"I phoned the hospital and explained what was happening but they wouldn't come. They thought it was an abortion.

"And in those days, abortion was so frowned upon they refused to assist.

"At the time we were living near the Turkish embassy, and there was a young copper there."

At this stage Jean was in agony lying in a pool of blood and Alf was petrified and helpless.

In desperation, he approached the young officer and explained his wife's terrible predicament.

"Can you please help us. We're desperate," he implored.

The pair ran back the 50 yards or so to the Bicknells' house. When they got inside Jean was doubled up in agony.

Alf said: "No-one will help. They won't send anybody round. There's something seriously wrong here."

The policeman grabbed the phone, hurriedly dialled and barked some orders down the line. The voice of authority did the trick and an ambulance arrived minutes later.

"I followed in the Beatles' car. The ambulance took Jean to the St Mary's Hospital in Paddington.

"They wheeled her in on the stretcher and the doctors got to work.

"I was told later that another 10 minutes without medical attention and Jean would have died.

"I stayed with her all day. It turned out to be a miscarriage, after all.

"Jean had about three or four miscarriages, although thank goodness we have one lovely son.

"But it wasn't something I felt I could discuss."

So the next day it was business as usual.

"I never talked about it with the band. From that day to this they didn't know the trauma my wife and myself had been through."

CHAPTER THREE
*The Shooting Of **Help!***

THE shooting of the film **Help!** was a particularly magical time for Alf during his years with the band. He saw another side to the group, which had not previously been in evidence. Away from the harsh gaze of public scrutiny and the mind-numbing effects of the touring and ever-screaming fans, the band were more relaxed. Indeed, the long breaks during filming provided the perfect antidote to life on the road, where practically every minute was spoken for.

This was the middle of February 1965. Ringo had married Maureen, and Paul, who had been on holiday in Tunisia with Jane Asher, had missed the wedding.

Like so many close to the band, Alf was convinced McCartney would tie the knot too, with Jane.

Prior to the bass player's departure for Tunisia, Alf had gone round to the Ashers, where Paul was staying, to help him pack.

He noticed how fond Mrs Asher – she of the legendary cooked breakfasts – was of her daughter's pop star boyfriend.

"I remember thinking how lucky Paul was. Mind you to see his room, you wouldn't think he was this famous star," smiles Alf.

"Paul never had much of his own stuff there – he lived very simply with little clutter.

"But he was really spoilt by Mrs Asher. And I definitely thought at that time, while they were in England to film **Help!**, that I would be asked to help Jane and Paul house-hunt."

Prior to the actual shooting of the film, Alf would ferry the group back and forth from the studio, where they would record tracks for **Help!**

During these sessions Alf noticed George Harrison's confidence in his own songwriting abilities growing.

"He was always a bit shy with his efforts, obviously it can't have been easy with Paul and John coming up with all this amazing stuff."

Lennon's ever-mercurial temper took a

turn for the worse.

The group were recording a new track, "Yes It Is", and despite repeated attempts, it just wasn't coming together, much to John's annoyance.

Eventually he snapped, a torrent of swearing filled the air, as he flung his guitar down, kicking a chair over as he exited the studio.

"They were getting awards from EMI in the presence of the record company's chairman Sir Joseph Lockwood that day, and I think we were all a bit worried about what John might do, given his outburst in the studio," he says.

"Thankfully they were good as gold – very little fooling around – and John was quite subdued. Anyway, Eppy was very pleased with them."

The interior shots for the **Help!** movie, which began filming in late February 1965, were filmed, in the main, in Twickenham studios. Location shots were filmed in a variety of colourful locations around the globe, such as the Bahamas and Austria.

At home, the boys filmed in and around

London. A great deal of external footage for the production was filmed on Salisbury Plain. Alf joined the cast and crew at a hotel, the Antrobus Arms in Amesbury, for a few days at the start of May, while these sequences were being shot.

"All of us, the cast and the band, were staying together in the hotel," says Alf. "There were people like Leo McKern, Victor Spinetti – a wonderful man – Eleanor Bron, Roy Kinnear, and so on."

Alf would be on hand as the group shot some of the film's outdoor sequences on Salisbury Plain. Despite the fact it was early May, the weather was distinctly cool and he was glad when each day's filming was over, and he and the rest on the entourage would head back to welcoming warmth of the Antrobus.

"It was bloody freezing cold out on Salisbury Plain and we'd be there for a good eight or nine hours a day. So I'd be on hand to take the boys hot tea, or sandwiches between takes.

"The Austin Princess would always be parked nearby, and it would be loaded up with little things that might be needed. There was everything there from aspirins and plasters to cigarettes and magazines. It was like a mobile shop.

"We'd have dinner after the shoot. A couple of tables would be pushed together and this wonderful ensemble of artists would hold court regaling each other with stories till the wee small hours.

"Eleanor Bron was an expert at telling tales, acting everything out; she had everyone in stitches."

The all-important card set was always brought out and Ringo, Leo and Alf provided the central core of the nightly poker sessions.

McKern proved to be the canniest poker player, repeatedly fleecing Alf or whoever was foolish enough to take him on.

"Leo must have made a fortune – from me alone."

Another sequence for **Help!** was supposed to take place at Buckingham Palace, and although filming outside didn't prove to be a problem, there was no chance that the rock and rollers would be given permission to film inside. So a suitable location had to be found to pass for the interior shots of the palace.

The perfect location was found at the magnificent Cliveden House in Berkshire, which was then the home of Lord and Lady Astor.

In May the **Help!** crew spent two days filming what turned out to be the last shots for the film here, which was the scene of Christine Keeler's infamous first meeting with Profumo.

"They were doing sequences, which were supposedly inside Buckingham Palace. One day, during this particular shoot, I remember one of the film crew made a comment about the fitness of the Fab Four to George," says Alf.

"It was a sort of jokey remark but very much a come-on to the boys, suggesting they were out of shape."

The gauntlet was thrown down, and The Beatles vowed to prove him wrong. "These jibes and come-ons continued, and over lunch it was suggested we have a relay race.

"So it was all set up. We were on a huge great lawn in front of Cliveden House – 150 yards long, or thereabouts with a privet hedge round it.

"The team was the four boys, plus Neil

and I. The six of us. I was to be on the last leg of this relay race against the cream of the film crew."

He dreaded letting his bosses down. "I guess we each had 70 or 80 yards to race against the electricians, the photographer, transport and so on. Four or five teams.

"There was a baton – a small truncheon. The first racer would run, pass it on and the next would sprint off and so on."

Alf quivered as he waited for his turn.

"Remember, I'm 35 years of age. I looked at the guy I was racing against and he looked very confident. I remember I was running barefoot, whereas he had a smart pair of sports shoes on. That didn't help my confidence."

The constant touring had obviously had a positive effect on the band physically, who proved to be superfit.

The four group members were to run before Alf and Neil, and they certainly gave their employees an incredible advantage over the opposition.

John, Paul, George and Ringo trounced the other teams during their leg of the race, leaving their opponents breathless in their wake as they delivered the baton to each other after their respective stints.

"Neil was to pass the baton to me. To be fair, the five of them had given me a tremendous start. The Beatles team were WAY out in front."

Neil flew towards Alf and passed over the baton and the chauffeur took off.

"Towards the end of my sprint, the last part of the race, as I reached a sort of steep banking slope at the end of the lawn, I could hear this guy behind me – he'd made up all this lead the boys had given me."

But the chauffeur was determined not to let the band down. He threw himself over the last few metres and stumbled over the finishing line, seconds before the other racer.

"We'd won! The band were soon all round me basking in their victory.

"It was only then I thought of what would have happened if I'd lost after all this space they'd given me. I'd never have heard the end of it.

"The Scouse humour would have been particularly cutting.

"But we'd won and we were presented with a beautiful crystal vase by Lord and Lady Astor. I think Paul took that."

By this time The Beatles' firm trust in Alf was palpable.

"It was creeping in. I could feel it," he reveals.

He had been given a clear example of the faith the band had in him. He was driving the group from Amesbury in Wiltshire to Salisbury Plain to film a scene for **Help!**.

The chauffeur had noticed in the rear view mirror that Lennon was watching him intently.

John's had a mischievous glint in his eye. Then, without warning, he leapt into action.

Suddenly he jumped forward and grabbed Alf's uniform cap.

He tossed it through the window.

The startled driver watched helplessly as the hat flew frisbee-style across the road.

Speechless, he wondered if he had done something wrong and this de-capping signified the end of the road as chauffeur with the group. But he needn't have worried.

John beamed: "Don't worry Alf, you don't need that any more. You're one of us now!"

Lennon was clearly speaking for the rest of the band, who all looked on, grinning at Alf, who now had been completely accepted as one of the close-knit Beatles' inner sanctum.

He recalls: "For him to say that meant a lot to me. I was very emotional – but I daren't have showed it. They'd immediately have taken the Mickey."

Lennon again honoured the driver some days later on yet another trip to Salisbury Plain.

Again he sat in the back of the car staring at Alf. There was obviously something on his mind.

He leaned forward and asked: "D'you wanna come on tour with us to America?"

Alf smiles: "I had no hesitation. With John you only got one chance and then the matter would be forgotten, never to be repeated. I said: 'Yes!' immediately.

"I felt it was such an accolade. I was exploding inside with excitement."

CHAPTER FOUR
American Dream

BEFORE he could set off on the American tour, Alf had to get hold of an International Driving Licence and a new passport. The previous one had expired long ago. The boys sat around while he filled in the form in the back of the car. "I remember coming to the bit which asked for occupation and saying, 'Guys, can anyone spell chauffeur?' Paul nudged me and said: 'Occupation, is that what they want to know? Put Musical Director'.

Alf flashed him an incredulous look: "Yeah right. How do you spell chauffeur?"

"Then we all headed for, what was then the BOAC in Victoria, to have our jabs.

"That was such a magical moment. There I was with The Beatles getting our injections. Neil and Mal, too. They were larking about as ever. There were other stars there like Acker Bilk getting his jabs too.

"And then off to America."

At midday on August 13, 1965, The Beatles left from Heathrow airport, with the sound of a thousand screaming fans still ringing in their ears.

Earlier in the day, Alf had said his goodbyes to Jean and son, Mark, who couldn't quite understand why he had to go.

"Mark was a bit upset at seeing Daddy off, but I promised to bring him back loads of great toys from the States and that seemed to cheer him up.

"It was a real whirlwind of a day. Myself and the others spent the morning preparing our baggage and making sure it got to the airport.

"We left Heathrow about noon. There were thousands of fans to see us off and in a way that was a rather poignant moment for me. A real show of support for John, Paul, George and Ringo as they set off for America.

"It was so exciting. Here I was, this 35-year-old who was relatively new to all this, and I was leaving London for the States with The Beatles.

"It was beyond my wildest dreams."

And as with everything else the group did, things were far from dull during the journey.

"Ordinarily, a long flight like that might be kind of dull, but not with the band – it was non-stop, card games, loads of booze, but above all laughter and joking."

A few hours later, Alf had dozed off. The others followed soon after.

Alf awoke and noticed that the group, along with Neil and Mal, were crowded against the windows, pointing out. The plane was landing at Kennedy International Airport and already they could make out a scene not dissimilar to the airport they had left.

Beatlemania Stateside.

"The whole airport was alive with thousands of screaming fans, waving at our plane.

"We were also being met by what seemed like the entire American media – newspaper reporters, TV interviewers, radio DJs.

"The plane landed safely – it was mid-afternoon – but there were problems on the ground. The controllers at Kennedy refused to let the group use the main building.

"This was infuriating for the band. Much as fans could be a somewhat hazardous prospect en masse, the group had been keen to at least get close to their followers in America."

But this was not to be. The airport authorities sent out limos to take them away, without them entering the main building.

Epstein had a brief word with his peeved charges and that seemed to do the trick. The group sped off in the limos... a different breed of vehicle to what Alf was used to.

"They really know how to make cars over there. These were glorious long stretch cars. It was a bit like being in a coach.

"From there we were escorted through the city in a convoy of cars with outriders, motorcyclists and so on, which whizzed us off to the Warwick Hotel."

The band took residence there, more than 30 floors up, for the next few days.

Needless to say, they were joined during their stay by the cream of the showbiz world.

"It was a constant stream of superstars. The Supremes one minute, Bob Dylan the next.

"One guy who struck me as being very

friendly was the actor Brandon De Wilde, who played the young boy in **Shane**. He came along with his wife."

Everything in America seemed bigger – even the press conferences. The same day they landed they faced their biggest ever gathering of the media.

"The boys were seated at a table, with dozens of microphones; the wall behind them and what seemed like hundreds of faces in front of them."

Beatles' spokesman Tony Barrow fielded the questions.

One hack asked if they had enjoyed their reception and John grumbled about not being able to meet the fans and his annoyance at having to disembark in the middle of an airfield.

Ringo enthused about the police escort, which made him feel very important.

But it was Paul who showed real patience as reporters probed and probed about his relationship with Jane Asher.

"They were obsessed about finding out if he was going to marry her. But he kept his temper and laughed his way through it.

"Someone else asked if was true Bob Dylan was going to meet with them and John said he thought it was going to be that night.

"This seemed to please the assembled journalists. One of their own pop stars meeting with The Beatles seemed significant, somehow."

Eventually tiredness prevailed and the conference came to an end, and the boys headed up to their rooms.

But sleep was not on the agenda just yet. There was a stream of guests, including, as predicted, Bob Dylan and The Supremes.

"When Dylan did show up, rather than be the awkward difficult artistic type his press would have had me believe, he was actually very approachable – friendly even."

But Alf's thoughts were elsewhere – London, with Jean and little Mark.

"I asked John if I could phone Jean and he told me of course I could. But I checked with Eppy anyway, who was fine about it too. I think he could see I was quite anxious to make sure they were OK in my absence.

"I remember I got Jean out of bed, I'd completely forgotten about the time difference.

"I must have ranted on about the incredible day I had. But after I hung up I realised how much I missed her and Mark."

Alf woke early the next day. He was sharing a room with Neil and Mal, a couple of doors down from the rest of the band. The Beatles had taken over the whole floor for security reasons and would remain there until August 17.

There were guards posted at the elevators.

Alf joined John, Paul and the others for a hearty breakfast. Their first performance was later that day – for the *Ed Sullivan Show*.

This was at New York's Studio 50. Again, much to Ringo's bemusement, the group were given a police escort to go to the mid-morning rehearsal, for the show which was to be recorded that night.

"Entire streets had to be closed as we passed through. Crowds of fans lined the road, pointing, shouting and waving as we drove past.

"It was electric – a great feeling."

At the studio Alf watched as the group ran through half a dozen numbers, including

"Ticket To Ride", "I Feel Fine" and a solo Paul singing "Yesterday", to a backing tape of violins.

"The audience – there were about 700 there – went berserk, there was no question of having some warm-up guy telling them to scream. They did that voluntarily. In fact, you couldn't have stopped them," laughs Alf.

"They worked really hard that day. They were obviously keen for everything to be spot-on. Brian and the band watched playbacks of the songs over and over again.

"The opener, 'I Feel Fine', was really powerful-sounding. I felt a bit for Ringo, who had to perform his new song, 'Act Naturally'.

"He said he was very nervous to the crowd and he clearly was. He needn't have worried. He seemed to have a huge following in the States and the fans were really behind him, as were the rest of the band providing backing vocals."

Neil, Mal and Alf took a wander round the studio. Security seemed even tighter than usual.

Ed Sullivan was polite but perfunctory, greeting the trio with a convivial, "Hi".

Alf sampled some of the food laid on and, deciding it fell short of what he had come to expect at the Warwick, headed back to watch the boys in performance.

Lennon, midway through "Help", was struggling – or perhaps obstinately refusing – to sing the right words, something which Alf had noticed happened frequently.

Lennon was ambivalent as he strolled offstage, "It doesn't matter," he said, "They should keep that in the show."

Alf's role with the band had developed somewhat from his driving duties.

"There was Neil, who was their personal roadie, Mal, who looked after the guitars, and me... so I was sort of number three.

"It was hard work but very exciting. While we were at the Warwick I made sure the guests were kept fed and watered. It was a question of looking after everyone."

He would tend bar, ensuring the stream of celebrities always had their glasses charged as they chatted to John, Paul, George and Ringo.

Again Alf would take the "just out of camera range" approach, keeping a discreet distance but always near enough, should anyone need his help, or – god forbid – if there was any trouble.

One night during the American tour he was to discover just what lengths a Beatles fan would go to be in the company of their favourite moptop.

Most of the guests had dispersed, either staggering off to adjoining rooms or speeding off in giant chauffeur-driven cars.

It was about 2.30AM, when Alf decided to call it a night himself.

Carefully closing the recreation room behind him, he headed wearily down the hall to his own quarters.

Exhausted, he pushed open his door, blissfully unaware and unprepared for what was waiting for him.

"When I opened the door, sitting in the chair was this beautiful redhead – 20, maybe 21 years of age she must have been," Alf recalls.

At first, he couldn't really figure out what was going on... then realisation dawned on his exhausted brain.

Alf looked straight at the beautiful

stranger, who by now realised herself that her plan of bedding a Beatle had gone horribly wrong. Wearily he said: "Tough! I'm afraid you chose the wrong room."

He laughs: "I've never figured out how she got through all the security up all those floors and into my room. It was amazing.

"She told me she'd travelled miles to see the band and she was clearly in a bit of a state. I was so tired I didn't want to argue."

He was tempted to turf her out of the room but he took pity on this flame-haired groupie, although there was no question of any hanky panky.

Jean would have killed him.

He decided to let her stay the night – although he made it clear they would have separate sleeping arrangements.

"I let her have my bed and I slept in a chair."

It was magnanimous gesture, but one which could have had very serious repercussions – the Press would have leapt on such a potentially salacious scoop connected with The Beatles.

Even one involving their humble chauffeur.

Fortunately, the rest of the night passed without incident, Alf curled up in the armchair and the Beatles-obsessed young lady tucked up in his bed.

The next morning she slipped discreetly from his room and Alf decided to come clean over breakfast.

The Beatles had their suspicions and were having none of it as he protested his innocence: "Come on, Alf, you must have done more than that. Come on, tell us," laughed a sceptical John.

"You seriously expect us to believe you had this gorgeous girl in your room – ALL NIGHT – and nothing happened?"

But Alf insists: "There was nothing more to tell. I often wonder where she is today and if she tells the story of the night she spent in the room with a Beatles roadie."

On August 15, The Beatles were to play their biggest ever concert. More than 55,000 fans were there to see them perform at New York's Shea

Stadium. The concert set new records both for attendance and profit.

But again the authorities fell foul of the Fab Four, when they refused to allow them to fly directly to Shea Stadium by helicopter, as they had planned.

"There was a great deal of discussion, phone calls flying back and forth between Eppy and the authorities but to no avail.

"In the end we were taken by limos from the hotel on 54th Street down to a heliport on the waterfront. From there we all clambered aboard a helicopter which took us right across New York. Hardly a word was spoken as we all gazed open-mouthed at the spectacle of the city below us.

"We flew right up to the World's Trade Fair on top of the Pan Am building. From there we were ushered into the lifts and right down to the ground.

"A magical mystery tour indeed. I kept trying to guess where we would be going next or what we would be travelling in."

The next mode of transport turned out to be an armoured truck, complete with armed guards.

"We all piled in and this took us to the Shea Stadium."

Already the noise was deafening as the fans waited for the arrival of the Fab Four.

Backstage the boys chilled out before the show, sprawled over sofas chatting to folk wandering in and out, while Mal carefully tuned the guitars.

As always Alf was on hand as and when he was needed.

He offered to help carry the gear onstage.

He picked up two guitars and followed Mal out of the dressing room.

"We went down this long winding corridor and into a tunnel. Then seconds later we were in the open air. That's when it hit us," recalls Alf.

"This wall of noise. It was so loud, it was physical. You could feel the excitement of these 50,000 fans as Mal and I ran to the stage to put the guitars on the stage."

The crowd went crazy, seeing these two distant microscopic figures, who were running toward the stage clutching guitars.

They presumed Alf and Mal were half of the Fab Four.

The roadies kept their heads down and hurtled towards the stage, not stopping to pay any heed to the frenzied reception.

Still panting from the run and shaking with nerves at his surroundings, Alf jumped on the stage and decided to leave Mal to deal with the technical side of things, now the thousands of fans had realised they weren't the stars of the show.

"I left the two guitars and headed back to the dressing room."

When he arrived back in front of the band, Alf was still visibly shaken by his first encounter with Beatlemania Stateside.

"What's up, Alf?" said George.

"Well, the place went mad at the sight of your guitars – lord knows what'll happen when the four of you go out there."

Soon, the boys slipped into their smart stage jackets and after chatshow king Ed Sullivan's introduction they headed out to face the music.

If the wall of sound had been deafening before, the crescendo now reached an almost physical fever pitch.

Alf, laden down with towels, headed to the left of the stage and watched as the boys rocked the home of the New York Mets.

It was a show which set new world records for a rock concert, twice over.

The sheer scale of the audience and the profits yielded from the performance were the biggest ever.

But to Alf, it was just another show as the group trotted out well-established favourites like "Twist And Shout", "I Feel Fine" and "Can't Buy Me Love" to the adoring but as ever, seemingly unlistening throng.

The screams were, indeed, he noticed a few decibels louder than the music.

The tour continued. An indoor show at Maple Leaf Gardens in Toronto, a performance in front of 30,000 at the brand new Atlanta stadium in Georgia, and two sets in one day, August 20, in Chicago's White Sox Park.

Backstage in Chicago, there was the

usual gathering of celebrities and civic officials. Centre stage amongst the throng was a man of the cloth, who was regaling all with his near-the-knuckle humour.

"This little Irish priest appeared. I think he must have had Liverpool connections. This guy had a huge repertoire of blue jokes that I don't think I've heard before or since," recalls Alf.

"He kept the band enthralled with his salty humour."

While they were listening to his gags, another religious figure entered the room. A monk complete with long flowing cowl came into the dressing room, his face completely submerged in a hood.

"It was surreal. You had this priest telling these jokes and a hooded monk."

Suddenly the monk raised his hands and dramatically swept back his hood.

"It was John Sebastian of the Loving Spoonful. He'd managed to walk through all the fans without any hassle. As John Sebastian he'd have been torn apart, he'd have been mobbed."

Between their show at Oregon's

Memorial Coliseum on August 22 and Balboa Stadium in California on August 28, The Beatles had nearly a full week off.

They took over a large house in Benedict Canyon, in Hollywood.

"Of course, they'd been in the States before and knew the drill but for me this was all completely new. We left the airport and drove into the Hollywood Hills," Alf recalls.

"I remember driving up to this beautiful house where we were going to stay. As we arrived in front of the building, the limo's doors opened and 'whoosh', the car was suddenly empty and I was there on my own.

"In just seconds, everybody had disappeared into the house."

Alf headed inside and couldn't see anyone.

Gradually the various Beatles began surfacing from different doorways.

"What's your room like, George," said John.

"Brilliant, what about yours?"

The band had used the first dibs principle to bag the best rooms, unfortunately for

Alf.

There was a little bungalow up the driveway, where Mal was going to stay. Neil was staying in another outhouse.

"We were basically a bedroom short – and guess who had drawn the short straw? I ended up sleeping in the games room.

"There were pool tables and card tables and so on. It meant I had to wait until everyone had gone to bed before I could get any sleep."

The Benedict Canyon retreat allowed the band to relax in style. There were two maids, a chef, and a butler called Roy.

"The Beatles knew all of them from the year before. A catering company had carefully selected them.

"Everything was laid out. Every morning breakfasts would be prepared but they were seldom eaten – everyone slept late."

For the next few days the entourage used the retreat to relax as they were pampered by Roy and his aides. Lunchtime to late afternoon was spent lazing by the pool. John, Paul, George and Ringo took the opportunity to go through some of the ever-growing mountain of mail.

"There was a stack of presents, gifts and letters which had been piling in," says Alf.

"Myself and Neil had the nightmare task of sorting it out but it was an impossible job. Just when you were beginning to get one lot in order, an even bigger pile would arrive.

"The band would select a few letters to read, or open a couple of presents. And they'd occasionally play taped messages, which the fans had recorded for them. John would usually get bored of this and start altering the speed of the tapes, so these voices were either going really slow or *Pinky & Perky*-style fast.

"He'd say, 'Actually I think it sounds better that way'!"

Some of the more creative fans would actually pen their own ditties, obviously hoping The Beatles might consider using their material.

The reality was very different.

"Paul and John would listen to these songs folk sent in. And to be fair, they'd try singing along with the choruses and so on.

"But it was just larking around – nothing serious."

All the while, Ringo and George would

be sunbathing, oblivious to the carry-on.

On August 24, the boss of Capitol records, The Beatles' record company in America, Alan Livingstone, threw a party.

It was decided that Alf would accompany Paul to the lavish do.

"I was a sort of chaperon, I guess you could call it, at this sort of do, and there was this trick I use to have to do, so whoever I was looking after – Paul in this case – wouldn't be caught in any compromising situations.

"Obviously there were always people desperate to have the band round for dinner, or to go out for a drink with one of them, but it was just not possible. Both for time and security reasons.

"The problem was people like Paul found it very hard to say 'no' to these people – that's where I came in.

"Someone would come up and go, 'You must come round for dinner, Paul,' or 'I'd love to show you round town tomorrow night', and it could potentially have been very awkward for Paul.

"So I would whip out this little diary and

flip through it, saying, 'Let's see – No forget it Paul, it's just not possible' and the matter would be closed, with Paul still very much the good guy."

The Capitol Records bash was probably the most star-studded event Alf had ever attended.

"The Beatles were always surrounded by celebrities but this was amazing even by their standards," he recalls.

"As we walked in, Dean Martin waved hello and I noticed Groucho Marx deep in conversation. Rock Hudson, Gene Barry, Edward G. Robinson, Jack Benny – Hollywood's A-list players were all there."

Alf stood with McCartney, as he chatted to a group of guests.

"I remember thinking, *Christ, here I am, a chauffeur from London, and here I am hob-nobbing, drinking the best wine, eating the finest food.* I was really buzzing inside."

Then he noticed another Hollywood legend surrounded by hangers-on.

"I'd always been a big fan of James Stewart. Years earlier I'd chauffeured a business colleague of his called Kirk Johnson, who'd told me what a wonderful man he was. Mr Johnson, who had died the year before, had been involved with a big oil company. I don't know if he and Jimmy Stewart were business partners but there was definitely a link there.

"I was keen to meet him, so I signalled to Paul to see if he would be alright on his own and he waved me off."

Alf approached the **It's A Wonderful Life** star, who was with his wife, and explained who he was.

Stewart turned out to be as charming as Alf had been led to believe, although the people around him seemed less than impressed with the Beatles' chauffeur.

Sensing their frostiness, the actor's wife invited Alf to dinner, but he declined.

"I'd love to but Brian Epstein would never give me the day off!" he laughed before turning to the snooty Hollywood luvvies and trumpeting triumphantly:

"Sorry to have interrupted."

Back at Benedict Canyon, the group – still buzzing from the party – stayed up for a while longer watching movies and drinking.

"I think we got through most of **What's New Pussycat?** and **Cat Ballou**, before we crashed out, exhausted."

As ever, security was tight at the Beatles' Stateside retreat, although this didn't stop the more ingenious fans attempting to reach their idols.

All day and night teenage girls could be spotted camped out in the hills surrounding Benedict Canyon. Some would wave frantically every time their heroes moved, while others would fight over binoculars to try and get a closer look at the band.

One hot afternoon as the entire entourage lazed by the pool, the buzz of a helicopter could be heard in the distance.

The craft drew closer until it was hovering above the house.

Then slowly the 'copter descended, until it was some four or five yards above the swimming pool.

To the amazement of the bemused and not a little frightened onlookers, the helicopter's doors flew open.

Within seconds, three female fans dived out, splashing noisily into the pool.

"It was a complete waste of time. Moments later Mal, Neil and I had dragged them out and were marching the soaking trio through the house out of the front door, where security escorted them off the grounds."

And another unexpected visitor to the Beatles' holiday home arrived later in the week.

"Obviously people came and went, musicians like Bob Dylan, Joan Baez or film actors like Eleanor Bron and so on. We were getting almost blasé about all these celebrities as we sunbathed by the pool," laughs Alf.

Then one day Mal sat bolt upright as a tall stranger approached.

He looked like he'd seen a ghost.

"What's up with you?" asked Alf.

"It's the Colonel."

Brian Epstein had just walked in with Colonel Tom Parker. The pair were trying to arrange for The Beatles to meet the King.

CHAPTER FIVE
An Audience With The King

AUGUST 27, 1965 was arguably the most remarkable day in Alf's entire time with the band – it was the one and only time The Beatles would meet, chat and perform with Elvis Presley. The day had started off innocuously enough. In the morning Alf'd popped out with Paul to do a bit of sightseeing. Macca had on one of his disguises, which usually involved a great deal of facial hair. This time, to be fair, he seemed to have pulled off the deception, Alf noticed. Paul slipped passed the security guards, none of whom seemed to recognise him.

"I remember I told them I was going with one of the catering staff – this was actually Paul – to pick up some food and other groceries. They seemed to accept this as they nodded and let us on our way.

"There would have been no way that would have happened if they had realised it was

Paul. But we had to keep our sightseeing trip mercifully brief. We wanted to be back for mid-afternoon to catch up on some sleep before the big night ahead.

"We were to meet Elvis at 11PM, so it was important that we were well rested."

Much has been said about the night the Fab Four met the King in Beverly Hills. Since no photographs were taken and the supposed tape recording of the meetings has never surfaced, most of the accounts are based on sheer speculation. Some reports say there was a highly competitive rift between Lennon and Presley.

That the latter deeply resented these new kids on the block and was deeply worried he would be de-throned as the King of rock and roll.

Other versions suggest John, Paul, George and Ringo found Elvis to be, well, boring. Alf Bicknell tells a different story.

"We arrived in this huge Cadillac. There were the four Beatles, Mal, Ian Brian, a guy called Chris Hutchins, who was working for the *New Musical Express*, and Tony Barrow, the

EMI man who was handling their publicity.

"There was about 10 of us who drove to Elvis' mansion in Perugia Way in Beverly Hills. As we arrived in the driveway, there was Elvis standing in the doorway grinning. He had on this magnificent red shirt and dark pants."

The King greeted each of the visitors as they clambered out of the Cadillac and made their way towards him.

Alf was last in line, but Presley greeted him graciously, with a firm handshake and the words: "Welcome to my home, sir."

Alf followed the others inside, with Elvis just behind him.

There was a magnificent hallway with an ornate fireplace in the centre of the room, with a copper chimney, which went straight through the ceiling.

To the far left was a pool table.

The party was led into an adjoining room, where there were large settees and three televisions flickering in the background, with the sound turned down.

Off to the right was a bar, where a group of people were gathered chatting, feigning disinterest in what they were witnessing – the most famous musical icons of their time gathered for the first – and what turned out to be the last – time ever.

As Paul and John sat down with the King, Brian Epstein and Colonel Parker looked on proudly, like two protective parents.

The room was about to witness the greatest musical line-up in pop history.

"Elvis reached behind where he was sitting on the couch and grabbed some guitars. He handed one each to Paul, George and John. Presley began strumming and the others began to join in, trying out different riffs.

"Ringo kept a sort of rhythm going on the side of the armchair. This went on for a short while.

"There was no singing, it was more a case of showing each other different guitar licks. Little blues riffs, a bit of 12-bar and so on.

"George would pick out intricate little melodies as this incredible band played their one and only gig together."

The impromptu jam session eventually petered out and everyone headed over to a bar in the far corner of the room.

Drinks were poured and Lennon challenged Elvis to a game of pool. George and Paul picked up their cues and a friendly game started. Meanwhile, Ringo had plumped himself down next to Alf to watch this clash of the pop titans on the pool table.

The chauffeur/roadie/personal assistant leaned towards the drummer and said: "You know I've been thinking, Ringo. Elvis is just one guy and he has about a dozen folk looking after him.

"Yet there's four of you and only three of us."

There was silence as Ringo considered the query before deadpanning: "Whatsa matter, Alf, d'you wanna raise?"

The matter was closed.

At one point during the evening, Alf was standing by a magnificent fireplace, watching the proceedings – people playing pool, shooting dice and so on – when The King, resplendent in his bright red shirt, came towards him.

He stood next to the awe-struck chauffeur and the pair watched the buzzing room together. "It's weird, I remember thinking, 'You're a big fellow, Elvis – but not as big as me.'"

Some four hours later The Beatles' party decided to head off. Elvis again shook hands affectionately as his visitors left for the journey back to Benedict Canyon.

"Since that day, there've been so many stories and rumours about that famous meeting. That it was awkward. That Elvis or John had been sarcastic to one another – but none of this is true.

"There were no photographs taken, which is a sad thing because it would have been wonderful to have Elvis and the Beatles pictured together.

"There were no recordings done when they played together but over the years people have gone on about John and Elvis not getting on.

"But there was nothing like that. All I remember was the great fun we had that day."

And The King had another treat in store.

Elvis sent his own roadies round in a giant Cadillac limousine to take the Beatles' road crew out on the town. Neil opted out but Alf and Mal had a whale of a time.

"We were wined and dined and went round all these wonderful Hollywood clubs.

"One place was closing for the night but Elvis' people Sonny and Marty had them open up just for us. Vintage champagne and platters of delicious food duly arrived.

"Then the singer who had been performing that night came back on and did another set, singing just for the likes of yours truly.

"I've always thought what a wonderful gesture of Elvis to have remembered us, the humble roadies, in this way."

Saturday, August 28, it was business as usual, with the first of the final four American dates. This was at Balboa Stadium.

The band seemed keen to be getting back to live work as they travelled to San Diego on a giant coach.

"This was more like a plane than a coach. Inside there were settees, a bar, rest rooms, cabinets full of drinks. There was still something of an afterglow in the wake of the Elvis meeting.

"I'd been stopped by a few DJs wondering if I'd been at this already legendary event, and it dawned on me what an incredible piece of musical history I'd witnessed."

The following two nights saw the Beatles perform at the Hollywood Bowl in Los Angeles.

"I remember a press conference before the first of these shows. This was at the Capitol Records tower and the band were given yet another award – a gold disc.

"One of the reporters mentioned that a fan had apparently had a baby during one of their shows in the States.

"The boys were quite impressed, although John assured the journalist they had no intimate knowledge of the young lady concerned."

Less amusing was security at the Hollywood Bowl.

Particularly after each show, when there was a 100-yard dash for the boys between the back of the stage and their awaiting cars.

"These were always frightening times.

This was when I had to really look after the band. With my arms in the air I'd run down, pushing off fans, protecting John, Paul, George and Ringo as we beat our way down the pathway.

"I remember I'd been given a lovely watch. At the Hollywood bowl this was snatched off me as we made our way through the crazed fans.

"I guess whoever took it thought they had a Beatles watch or something."

Alf was to meet another showbiz legend, as the band prepared for the final American concerts – two shows in one day at San Francisco's Cow Palace.

"This was a huge great arena the band were playing in and they had a suitably giant trailer backstage to relax in between the shows. I remember wandering back and I could hear music, an acoustic guitar being strummed.

"It was 'Greensleeves', and there was a woman half-singing, half humming along with the strummed chords.

"I quietly let myself in to the trailer and

stood by the bar which was inside... what a magical sight greeted me.

"There was George playing this ancient song, which Henry VIII had written all these years ago. Sitting next to him providing a beautiful vocal accompaniment was Joan Baez.

"I was enraptured, but then I was aware of another voice – a deep rich baritone coming from just beside me.

"I hadn't noticed him in the darkness of the trailer, but it was Johnny Cash. So I stood and listened as he harmonised with Joan, all the while smiling at me.

"I tried to savour this private concert these three legends were performing for me.

"The man in black by my side stopped singing and thrust out his hand. 'Hi, I'm Johnny Cash,' he said amiably, as if I wouldn't have known.

"Years later our paths crossed again at a fund-raising charity concert I was invited to in the mid-west of America.

"Johnny Cash and his family were principal guests. Backstage I approached him and said, 'This is very strange but almost 30 years ago we met–'. Before I could finish he interrupted, 'Sure, I remember – backstage Cow Palace, San Francisco – "Greensleeves", wasn't it?'.

"He remembered it well, and we recalled the old days as he signed a picture for me."

The actual Cow Palace concert was the scene of the most frenzied display of Beatlemania Alf had ever seen. There were two performances that day. A matinee in front of 11,500 and an evening performance in front of 17,000.

"All their shows were electric – I always had a tremendous buzz of nerves and sheer excitement as they took to the stage and I watched from the wings to be on hand should, god forbid, things get out of hand.

"But this was way different. The adrenalin level was a few notches higher. There was pandemonium in front of the stage as the boys took to the stage and picked up their instruments."

At one point the crush was so dangerous and life-threatening down the front that the group had to vacate the stage until some semblance of order was restored.

While the other three remained in their dressing rooms Paul returned and appealed to the fans to cool down a bit, to avoid anyone being hurt.

The concert resumed but there was another heart-jolting surprise for Alf. A fan appeared as if from nowhere backstage. He'd obviously managed to get through the tight security somehow, and was now making his way across the studio determined to bag himself a memento of his brief appearance onstage with the greatest pop band in the world.

His eye caught John Lennon, or more specifically, Lennon's beloved sailor's hat, which he liked to wear onstage.

"In one sort of single-bounce movement, this guy had whipped it off the stage and dived back into the audience."

It had been so quick, Alf was helpless to intervene. Miraculously the hat was returned back to the stage a few minutes later – much to Lennon's delight.

The stage invasions continued and Alf had to keep rushing on to carry off hysterical fans.

"I'd been on for 'Yellow Submarine', when I sang along with the rest of the band on the backing vocals.

"But this was my one and only time onstage, so to speak, with The Beatles."

CHAPTER SIX
In The Studio

DURING Alf's time in The Beatles' employ, they recorded three albums: *Help!*, *Rubber Soul*, and *Revolver*. It was clear to the driver that they were happiest when recording. The frustrations of performing to fans who chose to scream rather than listen, coupled with the lack of time they had to write new songs while on the road, would eventually lead to them quitting live shows altogether. For Alf too, the halcyon days he spent playing cards with Mal at Abbey Road, with a soundtrack of the Fab Four recording nearby, are amongst his fondest memories of his time with them.

During their recording sessions Alf's remit required a lot more than chauffeuring the boys back and forth from the studio. He was on hand to fetch instruments, or make endless cups of tea for producer George Martin and the thirsty musicians.

He was also in charge of making sure the band were kept well-fed during the gruelling stints, which often ran on into the early hours. Alf was adamant John, Paul, George and Ringo should at least eat well, if they couldn't leave the studio. So, a nightly ritual developed.

He would drive round to a little Italian restaurant he had discovered, which was close to the Abbey Road studios, and pick up some menus. The owner, delighted he had such famous customers, was happy to oblige.

Alf would return to the studio and the band would eagerly pore over the menu.

They would tell Alf which dishes they wanted and carefully select a few choice wines. Paul often had a hankering for avocado vinaigrette, although Ringo's tastes were a bit simpler.

"Just make sure you don't get me anything with onions," he would say, as Alf headed off again into the night and the Fab Four, now hungrily anticipating their evening meal, went back into the recording studio.

Back at the restaurant, the chauffeur would wait while the dishes were prepared.

The owner would then carefully place them in a giant hamper together with cutlery, napkins and several bottles of wine.

Back at Abbey Road, Alf would carefully set up the table, placing four settings complete with finest silver service, napkins and crystal glasses.

He'd uncover the various dishes and uncork a few bottles of wine.

Then he'd watch for the all-important red light above the studio door to go out, signalling a break in the recording session.

The Beatles' impromptu waiter for the evening would then toss a towel over his arm, pull open the door and announce grandly: "Gentlemen, dinner is served!"

The group would emerge and feast their eyes on Alf's grand spread, as the chauffeur cracked open the wine.

As the band sat around the table, he'd fill their glasses and step back to let them enjoy the meal.

He'd look on fondly as the inevitable Scouse banter would fly back and forth across the dinner table, sometimes about the track they were currently recording, but more often than not about their lives outside the studio. Girlfriends, houses, cars they were thinking of buying, or Jagger, Dylan – whatever pop star they had bumped into that week.

A good half hour or so later, well-sated, the Fab Four would head back into the studio and the red light would once again beam down from above the door, as another future chart-topper was put together.

Alf was often privy to seeing the legendary Lennon and McCartney partnership doing what it did best – writing songs, most of which were destined to become 20th century classics.

"People often ask me if they would write stuff in the back of the car, or in dressing rooms. I don't know, to be honest. I certainly never saw that happen.

"In the studio, whoever had written the lyrics or the music, whichever was at the core of the song, seemed to take charge – that's the way it seemed to me."

As the Fab Four were locked away with producer George Martin at the helm, Alf and

Mal would be arguing over a game of cards or a relaxed chess session. Occasionally, one of the band would pop out and the duo would hear someone tinkering on a keyboard.

"They'd sit round the piano and I'd hear them planning 'Help!', 'Paperback Writer', 'I'm A Loser', or whatever. We sort of got used to hearing these amazing songs in their infant stages.

"We almost became oblivious to the fact that the greatest songwriters this century has ever seen were a few feet away from us creating these wonderful classics.

"Bear in mind they'd work for hours on end. Usually all day, and often right through the night."

But this nonchalance always changed when a track was in the can all ready for the final mix, and Mal and Alf were always invited to lend their ears to the creative process.

They leapt towards the control room with the others.

"We'd all trot up to the side stairs to the room where the mixing desk was," he recalls.

So Mal and Alf, aside from The Beatles

and George Martin, were the first to hear the initial takes of dozens of Fab Four classics.

"It was so exciting. To sort of observe them discreetly as they listened to the playback," he remembers.

"The intensity on the faces of John, Paul, George and Ringo as the tape played, was amazing, particularly of the Beatle whose composition it was."

But it wasn't just as an audience to these playbacks, that Alf was required.

He can be heard singing on one of their best-loved tracks, "Yellow Submarine".

"I was playing chess with Neil Aspinall, when they were doing the *Revolver* album. There was a cupboard in Abbey Road, which was used to store equipment for various sound effects, and so on.

"John asked us to fetch a few things for a song they were doing.

"Then Mal, Neil and myself were asked to help out with vocals on the chorus of 'Yellow Submarine'.

"Afterwards we headed up to the sound room to hear the take of our vocals."

PARTICULARS CONCERNING THE DRIVER

Surname. BICKNELL .. 1

Other names ALFRED GEORGE 2

Place of birth HASLEMERE SURREY.

Date of birth 28 . 10 . 28 .: 4

Home address 28 DEVONSHIRE CLOSE
LONDON W.1.

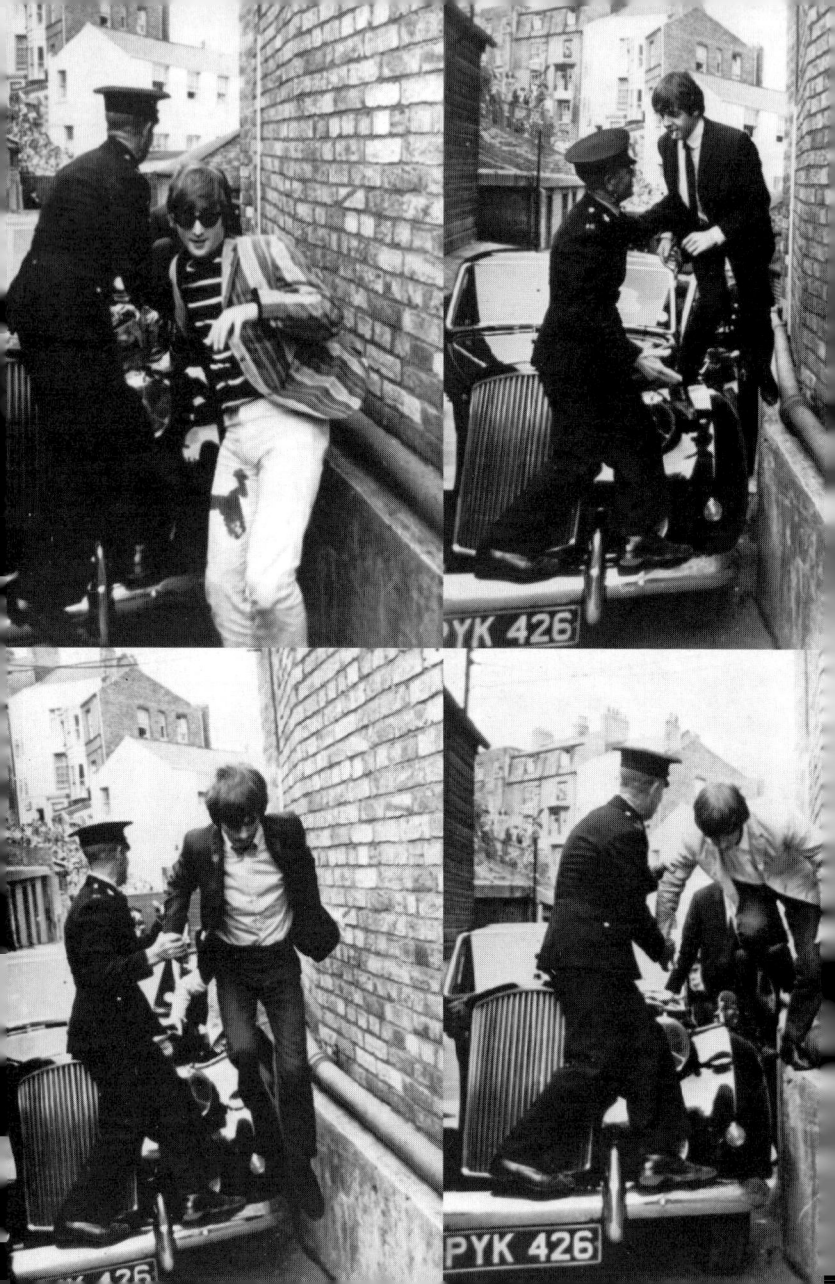

On another memorable occasion at Abbey Road, Alf was summoned by Lennon to provide the service of lyric sheet holder.

"I can still recall it so vividly, it was studio number two. John was in front of me, George was strumming away nearby and Paul was sat at the piano.

"They were doing this song and John just couldn't seem to remember the words. So he had scrawled the lyrics down on this crumpled brown envelope.

"The words were all over the place – first down one side, then across the bottom and then over the other side of it too.

"I had to hold it really close as he sung, as he was so near-sighted. As the track progressed, I was to turn the envelope to whatever bit John was singing.

"It was quite bizarre but very nerve-wracking for me. There I was in the middle of the studio with The Beatles and George Martin up in the control booth.

"Anyway, this cracked John up. He stopped the song midway and started grinning at me.

"He was laughing because my hand was shaking so much he couldn't read the words. Besides, John's handwriting was so messy, that the scrawl wouldn't have helped.

"'Look at the state of you, Alf,' he said, and he decided to try and find another way of reading his lyrics."

There's no disguising Alf's excitement as he speaks of being at the "birth of all this magic".

"I'm often asked what my favourite tracks are. I heard all of *Rubber Soul*, *Help* and *Revolver* coming together. *Rubber Soul*'s still my favourite. I'm biased, as it was a particularly fond time for me. Plus I was there when they had the cover done," he adds.

"I'm often asked what my favourite tracks are. I don't really know.

"I guess the two which I think are most poignant are 'Penny Lane' and 'Strawberry Fields Forever'. They make me really sad – I don't know why.

"It's weird to explain. Even after I left them in 1966 and went back to working with captains of industry and on a cruise, I could never get these songs – all their tracks – out of my system.

"They'd become a part of me. To be there was the job of a lifetime."

At the time he never realised the sheer future longevity of the band, or how valuable original Beatle gear would become.

"It wasn't until the '80s when I started attending conventions and seeing all these thousands of people and the kind of crazy prices being paid for things like the Butcher's sleeve, autographs, photos and to see all these bootlegs – it was a revelation."

CHAPTER SEVEN
Beatle Weddings

THE Beatles normally piled into Alf's Austin Princess to go off on tours, visit TV studios or take part in whatever high-profile media event they were asked to attend. This was fine. Alf had from his early time with the band, tried to ensure that some measures be taken to protect their anonymity as much as possible. He'd had all the windows blacked out, for example, and this generally threw even the most perceptive fans off the scent. But there were occasions during his three-year stint, that the Princess was simply too ostentatious.

Times when The Beatles insisted on having their space – their privacy. Alf was a key member of the team assigned to ensure the weddings of George Harrison and Ringo Star were kept as private as possible. Fans, and more importantly journalists desperate for a scoop, were to be kept at bay. On such occasions, the

---

chauffeur would leave the Princess in the garage and phoned up his old mates in the car-hire business. They'd fix him up with something a little less conspicuous.

"For George's wedding, I borrowed a small Honda car," recalls Alf.

"George and Patti were getting married at Epsom Registry Office. It was very quiet; Brian, Mal and I along with family and friends.

"The wedding went off without a hitch – few people knew about it. Like the rest of the entourage, I'd known about it for some time but we'd all kept it hush-hush. Although, as ever, the Press got wind of it and swamped us all at the registry office.

"After the registry office we drove back to George's house."

The reception and meal at the guitarist's home were trouble-free affairs and passed without incident.

"I'd always been very fond of Patti. I remember one time picking her up and I had my son Mark with me. He must have been three or four at the time, but already he seemed to have an eye for the ladies.

"I picked her up at George's house in Esher. And during the journey, Mark kept craning his head round to get a look at this beautiful lady. Little did I know what he had in mind.

"Suddenly Mark turned on the seat to face Patti, who was in the back seat.

"'Can I have a kiss?', he blurted out to my absolute embarrassment. I could have murdered him.

"She was so great about it. Laughing and giving him a peck on the cheek."

Prying eyes were unable to witness the low-key reception at George's house.

"He had huge wall – a good 12 or 14 feet – around it. His housekeeper – a lovely lady – had laid on a grand spread."

The guests mingled and chatted as the chauffeur waited for the appointed time to drive to the airport with George and Patti.

Then, when the newlyweds had spoken with all their in-laws, George signalled to Alf that the couple was ready.

"Let's go," he mouthed to his driver.

They were to be whisked off to the

airport, while their guests continued to celebrate the wedding at George's house.

"The three of us jumped into this small Honda saloon. While we'd been at the reception at George's house, it must have gradually filtered through to the Press about this Beatles wedding."

Journalists and photographers began to gather at various hideouts along the route from George's house to Heathrow airport. Within minutes of leaving the pop star's house, Alf had a trail of scoop-hungry hacks on his tail.

"These were very definitely not fans – these were journalists. We're on this stretch of road near Hampton and I hammered my foot down on the accelerator," continues Alf.

"We pass a bus stop and maybe two or three hundred yards later, a uniformed policeman steps out from behind a tree and waves us to stop."

Alf braked to a halt and emerged from the car, all the while mindful of the pack of baying pressmen on his tail.

The policeman informed him he'd been caught speeding.

"You've been caught in a speed trap

travelling in excess of the required limit," he told the driver.

Alf recalls: "A speed trap in those days was a copper in plain clothes in a bus stop using his instincts to judge if you were speeding. If you were, he'd jump out and wave a handkerchief to his colleague down the road.

"As the policeman – I always remember he was Welsh – was talking to me, I noticed all the cars following me had drawn to a halt back up the road. They could obviously smell a front page splash in the air."

Alf decided police help was badly needed.

He told the officer: "You see these cars up the road there. I'm trying to get away from them."

The officer was bewildered.

Alf stumbled on: "The couple in the back of the car have just got married and I'm trying to get them to the airport with the minimum amount of fuss. They're, erm, VIPs and these cars up the road there are full of reporters and photographers.

"That's why I had the foot down, I

wanted to try and give my passengers a little privacy."

The policeman, still trying to follow what was going on, shot back: "So who got married then. Royalty or a rock star?"

Bingo! The window on the car was pulled down and a familiar face popped out.

The officer's expression changed from annoyance to one of complete understanding.

But despite his sympathy towards Alf and his current dilemma, he had a problem. To openly let the Beatle's chauffeur off scot-free in front of Fleet Street's finest would probably see him booted from the force.

Then a brainwave struck him. He said to Alf: "Give me your licence."

Alf was crestfallen but the officer continued: "No, give it to me and I'll go through the motions so it looks like I'm booking you."

This piece of subterfuge acted out, the wily officer handed back Alf's documents, wished George and Patti all the best and the party were on their way again.

"But take it easy with the speed, eh?" he warned Alf.

He assured Alf he'd find some reason to hold the Press cars up for at least a few minutes, so he could make it to the airport without further problems.

"I drove away not too quickly until he was out of sight, and then I was off like the clappers. Soon we were on the concourse at Heathrow.

"Only one pic was taken, obviously by a guy on duty at the airport.

"All the Press people had been held up by this quick-thinking Welsh policeman, who I'll always be grateful to."

CHAPTER EIGHT
Drugs And Rock & Roll

IT'S no surprise that there's one subject Alf is
continually asked about regarding his time with
the Fab Four – the seamy side of The Beatles.
The hedonism, the orgies, the drug-taking. The
sexual experimentation – cocaine-fuelled trysts
with eager groupies. Let's deal with each of
these in turn, with the biggie first – The Beatles'
bonking. Alf, although quick to insist even if the
opposite were the case he wouldn't spill the
beans, says that there were was none. Well, very
little. The Beatles touring "machine" didn't allow
time for such diversions. Without denying that
the occasional tour fling – "they were young
guys after all" – may have taken place, Alf says
the band would never EVER have got intimate
with a fan, or God forbid, a groupie.

First off there was the fear of adverse
publicity, but furthermore the stringent security
surrounding them made such a dalliance

---

impossible.

Drug-wise, though, the band did choose to experiment during Alf's time in their employ.

The first whiff of illicit substances came very early on during his time with the band.

"At this stage, I didn't even have a car but was borrowing one to chauffeur them around. I'd picked up John, Neil was sat next to me and we went to George's house.

"George clambered in and I began to drive off. Then I noticed a burning smell. 'Something's on fire,' I said and stopped the car in the driveway.

"When I turned round John and George were in fits of giggles."

John told him: "There's nothing burning, Alf. It's just something in the ashtray. Don't worry about it."

Alf laughs: "Boy was I naive – but not for much longer. A few days later I visited Neil, who had a little place in the centre of London, and he gave me my first joint.

"I'll never forget. I'd be sat there going, 'This is rubbish, it does absolutely nothing for me,' one minute, then I'd be in fits of giggles the next.

"I sort of felt it was necessary for me to be cool about cannabis, if I was to be involved with the band closely.

"I treated it as just another aspect of the music business. But I never ever took any kind of drug, while I was chauffeuring the boys around."

Alf became used to seeing The Beatles when they were stoned. They were even more mischievous but there was never any real harm done.

"It was always silly pranks. When they weren't touring or recording they would party very hard. Some nights I'd bring them home from a club and it would be 5/6AM in the morning.

"One morning like that we were coming back from the Ad Lib club. We were coming off the Edgware Road. I knew London very well and would use back roads.

"We passed this dairy and there were crates of milk outside it. 'Stop Alf,' said John."

There was conspiratorial whispering and much hilarity, then Lennon piped up: "Wait there, we're off to get some milk."

Alf laughs: "I then saw one of the most surreal sights I have ever seen. Four of the most famous and richest musician stars in the land, furtively walking up to the dairy, then grabbing a pint of milk each.

"They jumped back in the car and Lennon shouted, 'Right Alf, let's scarper!' like they'd just robbed a bank or something – not pinched a couple of pints of gold top."

This was in the early days and I remember thinking: "What have I let myself in for?"

Prior to the American tour in 1965, Alf discovered he had a new role – as joint roller-upper.

Neil arrived at his door late at night with a carton of 12 boxes of cigarettes, a chunk of marijuana and some roll-up papers.

"He asked me to make up some joints for the tour. To be honest, I didn't really think about the consequences. Had I known how serious this was then, I'd never have agreed.

"Can you imagine what would have happened had I been caught?"

Alf had his work cut out for him. He'd take each pack of 20, split open the cigarettes, add the hash and re-seal them into joints.

For each pack of 20, an industrious Alf would replace the contents with 25 marijuana cigarettes.

"I sat up practically all night rolling joints for the American tour.

"I made them all and then carefully placed them in the cartons. Then I got the cellophane I'd peeled off and wrapped it back around the packs.

"Then I'd use a warm iron to seal the packs, as if they hadn't been opened. The next day I carried it to the airport under my arm.

"Neil had asked me to do it, so I just did it. I suppose in my own naive way I was happy to do it."

It was just another little Beatle chore. Little did he know that as a drug courier – carrying around hundreds of joints – he would have faced a lengthy spell inside if caught.

"In the '60s, can you imagine? I'd have probably been put away for 10 years," sighs Alf.

In hindsight, he is still a bit peeved that

Aspinall didn't warn him of the terrible consequences, if he'd been busted.

"That's what always bugged me. He never said a thing.

"I'd have been in serious trouble. I've often wondered if he thought that was funny in a perverse way."

The seriousness did hit Alf when the band had to travel up to Canada on the Stateside tour and he had to leave the dope behind.

"We were in Los Angeles and had to go up to the Maple Leaf Gardens in Toronto. I was very uncomfortable by this point carrying all these little natural smokes everywhere with me.

"There was absolutely no way that I was going to take them with me to Canada.

"I remember the person I left the joints with said to me, 'Yes, I'll do it – but don't ever ask me to do this again'.

"This was Wendy Hanson, who was Brian Epstein's personal assistant, who was an absolutely lovely lady and she was clearly angry at me for asking. I've regretted doing that ever since.

"I think it was then the seriousness of it

really hit home.

"Wendy reluctantly agreed to hang onto the joints till we returned from the Canadian concerts. I would pick them up from her when we met up again in New York."

He was also called on to perform a bizarre piece of subterfuge, when the group were enjoying a few joints at the various hotels they were staying in.

Obviously the whiff of cannabis would have been a dead giveaway, so Alf took to smoking big fat cigars near the doorway.

"I didn't even smoke cigars, but they were the only thing which I could think of to cover up the stench of the boys' joints.

"And it worked – no one was ever any the wiser."

When Alf arrived back in Blighty after the tour, he stepped off the plane, blissfully unaware the few remaining joints which he'd carefully stashed in his suitcase were about to be discovered by customs officials.

"Whenever we flew back home the plane doors were opened and – 'whoosh' – The Beatles were gone back to their various houses.

"I was left with all the luggage and when I got to the barrier the customs guy homed in on one suitcase."

Alf's suitcase. THE suitcase.

It contained some of his clothes, and the unwary drugs carrier had stuffed a few cannabis cigarettes between his shirts, in sleeves, and so forth.

"There's a famous picture by Bob Whittaker, which is of all the Beatles luggage and sitting right there in the centre is a black suitcase with a sort of silver strip round it.

"That's mine – the only one the customs picked on. I'd a few joints left so I'd thought if I just tucked them in my shirts which I'd had laundered, no one would be any the wiser."

Who knows why, but this was the item of luggage that stuck out to the customs men like a beacon.

They homed in on Alf's humble carrying case and took it to the side for closer examination.

The inquisitive customs official took hold of the case and snapped it open, probably drowning out the sound of its owner's gulp of terror.

"It was bizarre. There was all this luggage. All the Beatles' gear and all he was interested in, to my horror, was this little suitcase.

"I'll never forget it. He started flicking through my shirts and all these bits of joints were popping out everywhere," says Alf.

He dreaded what was about to happen and feared for the worst.

"To my amazement he just looked at me for a second, flipped the case shut again and said 'OK'."

"There's no question about it, he knew what I was carrying but he let me go. To this day, I'll never know why but, boy, was I grateful."

Alf, himself something of a novice when it came to imbibing illicit substances, began using marijuana during his time with The Beatles. Only on one occasion, however, did he take LSD, a move which was strongly opposed by Lennon, of all people.

The down side of the LSD tripping experience – particularly when the recipient is unaware of what's been taken – was encountered, all too vividly, one night when Alf was asked to chauffeur two of the Beatles to a posh dinner party in London.

"I had to drive John and Cynthia, along with George and Patti, to Hyde Park Square in London to this dental surgeon's place.

"They went in to dinner and I headed off to get something to eat. Fortunately, as it turned out, I got back pretty quickly and waited in the car.

"Suddenly they all ran out and jumped into the car and they seemed to be in a bit of a state.

"It was a strange but in some ways hilarious night. I was on the outside looking in and I didn't really know what was going on in their heads.

"This was not the John and George I was used to dealing with.

"But ultimately I was there to serve these people and take care of them."

They told Alf, the only straight one among them, what had happened.

"This man, this doctor had slipped LSD

into the coffee. And this was a professional man – a dental surgeon. I'm convinced this is the first time they had ever taken the drug.

"There are various stories surrounding this incident. That they went on to a club or that George was driving... not true. I can swear to that.

"They got in the car and were clearly quite distressed. They kept asking: 'What are we going to do?'"

Alf decided to drive them back to Esher to what Alf called the Wall Bungalow, George's house.

"I'll always remember, we were driving down the Kingston bypass, passed these rugby fields and on the left were all these tennis courts and so on.

"There is a section which is split by conifer trees pine trees and I remember one of the ladies, Patti saying: 'Look at these big brown bears. They are just so huge'. She must have been hallucinating like crazy."

A worried Alf pressed the foot down and they sped off towards the guitarist's house.

"They were screaming, 'Alf, don't go so

fast.' And I was like doing 30 mph, 40 mph, max.

"But I could tell they were getting very nervous, very agitated, so I slowed down even more."

He slipped out of the car pulled back the gate and drove his famous passengers up the driveway.

"I let them out and it was an unpleasant experience they were going through.

"They were still clearly under the influence of LSD, but back in the safety of George's place they seemed more relaxed.

"Patti looked out at George's swimming pool and said, 'Look, the swimming pool's turned completely red.'"

Alf remained till he felt it was safe to leave.

"After a bit, I decided it was safe to head off. I secured the door and left the four of them there. That was all that was ever said about that incident.

"I always thought what that doctor had done was despicable, lacing their coffee with this potent drug without their knowledge.

"They also took acid at Benedict Canyon in the States. Just after they'd taken it, a journalist arrived at the gates, and security weren't sure if they should let him in. But John said, 'No, let him come down to see us.'

"For some reason, John was adamant that I shouldn't take any LSD. John said once, that this – at Benedict Canyon – was the second time he had tried the drug, and I remember the occasion well.

"I don't know whether he was concerned over the effect it would have – but he didn't want me to do it.

"It was a beautiful afternoon and I think all the band had taken some LSD. They had a couple of pals there too, who'd dropped some acid as well. Even Neil had taken it – it seemed everyone was tripping except me.

"Then the nightmare scenario occurred. A message came through that the journalist, an English reporter, was at the gate for an arranged interview with the group.

"I was convinced they would refuse to meet with him, but John smiled and waved at me to go and let this fellow in."

The journalist was Don Short of the *Daily Mirror*.

"He was a really nice guy and I was dreading the whole thing. I wasn't sure if the boys were in a fit state to be interviewed. But I didn't say anything to Don."

The reporter sat by Paul and began asking questions.

"I can still picture Paul politely and carefully answering all these questions, desperately trying to look and sound straight, in control of himself – normal.

"To his credit, he carried it off. Don stayed most of the day as The Beatles became more and more stoned.

"They were larking about, laughing, giggling one minute, then staring intently at something the next.

"Don didn't twig what was going on. He obviously thought this was typical behaviour from those wacky loveable moptops. It was hilarious – boy, could he have a real scoop that day if he had realised."

But he remembers most of the "high" times with great fondness. Those occasions when he skinned up with some of the world's greatest recording artists.

"I was 35 years old. I don't think I really knew what cannabis was. Neil sort of turned me on to it."

On one occasion he and Paul decided to visit Bob Dylan – the man widely credited for introducing The Beatles to cannabis – who was staying at the Savoy Hotel.

Robert Zimmerman was holding court in his room, surrounded by the likes of poet Allen Ginsberg and Motown legend Dionne Warwick, when the chauffeur and his boss arrived.

"We get there and go up to Dylan's suite of rooms and immediately the joints are passed around," recalls Alf.

Several neutron bomb spliffs later and a few scotches and Alf begins to feel the effect, and sets off to look for his "own space".

"I took a large drink and a giant joint and headed off for a wander."

A clearly inebriated Alf staggered down the hallway, trying to take in his surroundings. The wallpaper, the ornate cornicing took on a whole new hue as he ambled along, whisky and giant joint in hand.

He poked around the various doorways, searching for that vital chill-out factor.

"In one of the bedrooms was this grand old Victorian wardrobe," he recalls.

Taking another toke on the joint and a thirsty slug on the whisky, Alf made for his nirvana – the wardrobe.

"I pulled open the door and climbed in, carefully shutting the door behind me.

"Minutes passed, maybe hours – who knows when you're stoned – but soon I wasn't alone in the room."

Bob Dylan and a famous British female folk singer had stumbled into the room and headed straight for the bed.

The pair started tearing at each other's clothes lustily, thinking they were alone.

The heat of passion was turned up a few notches as they tore into each other, oblivious that they had an, admittedly comatose, observer just several feet away.

Dylan was in the middle of a steamy clinch, when he noticed smoke seeping out of holes in the wardrobe. Realising he wasn't hallucinating Bob panicked and threw open the doors of the unit.

There he found a stoned and somewhat inebriated Beatles roadie smiling apologetically up at him.

Dylan grinned and said: "It's you, Alf. I thought the place was on fire, man."

Alf laughs: "I remember some years later telling that story to George Harrison and he said, 'You weren't there'.

"I said 'George, there was Bob, Allen Ginsberg, Dionne Warwick and me – YOU weren't there. We eventually agreed to differ and decided we'd been on different days to see Bob."

As for Dylan, Alf says: "People often say he's difficult to work with but he was great with me. Some time later he was staying at the Mayfair Hotel.

"Dylan had made a film and he was going to show it in the hotel, where there was a small cinema. I took the boys along to see this concert movie."

As they were going into the hotel a beaming Dylan stormed down the stairs, bypassing The Beatles and shouting at Alf. "You gotta see this."

Alf beams: "He was holding the picture of me running across the stage with the fan at Cow Palace – it was the first time I'd ever seen it.

"It struck me. There's this legend and he remembers a lowly figure like me. It was funny the way he ignored the Beatles at first, to show me this picture.

"Some years later in London I saw Dylan in Berkeley Square. He'd emerged from offices there and was chatting to someone.

"I toyed with the idea of going over to him to see if he still remembered me.

"But that was all in the past, so I turned and walked away."

CHAPTER NINE
France, The Negresco

OBVIOUSLY Alf was no stranger to working with celebrities. Already in just a few short years he had worked with the likes of David Niven, Sophia Loren, Peter Cushing and so forth, but undoubtedly his current remit was the most high-profile. There was one occasion, however, when his former role as a chauffeur to the stars had repercussions to his present job as chauffeur-cum-tour assistant to the biggest rock band in the world.

"The European tour was a joy. I'd sorted out my International Driving Licence, but Eppy didn't think I'd be doing much driving. It was more a case of me being on hand to help out Neil and Mal," says Alf.

"The first port of call was Paris, where we were staying at the Georges Cinq Hotel. The boys were playing a couple of shows at the Palais des Sports.

"Chris Denning came along to the hotel to interview them and that seemed to go quite well. He also got the four of them to dedicate a song to folks back in England.

"Neil even ended up being asked for a dedication."

After the interview, Alf got chatting with Chris in the hotel bar and the pair shared a few anecdotes.

"We arranged to meet later at a local club, Castell's. So we all headed there after the evening performance.

"It was a bit like a French version of the Ad Lib club, with the added bonus of the most delicious onion soup I've ever tasted."

The band were playing France and were staying at the Negresco Hotel at the time.

"It was a wonderful place. Every room was done out in a different time period," recalls Alf. "The room that I had was done out like a magnificent Arabian tent. On the night they arrived the boys had the evening off, so it was decided they would all go out for a meal.

"We were in France, and sampling the famous French cuisine was something the boys loved to do," says Alf.

The party – John, Paul, George, Ringo, Neil, Mal and Alf – congregated on their floor and set off out.

"We came down in the lift. All of us. There were two cars waiting outside for us," says Alf.

As he stepped out the chauffeur heard a voice. "Alf, Alf, Alf–"

It was one of David Niven's sons, desperately trying to get his attention. Alf had driven the gentleman film star on many occasions. Indeed, he was the chauffeur's favourite star.

Like most of his on-screen characters, Niven was the quintessential Englishman.

Well-mannered, polite and, despite his superstar status, down-to-earth, ego-free and lacking in any pretensions.

He would often have his family in tow.

Niven was never a problem to work with. Niven Junior, however, on this occasion in France, was determined to use his previous links with Alf to his advantage.

The youngster, like so many others, was

a Beatles fan and, needless to say, desperate to meet them. Alf, however, had never used his position as part of the Fab Four's inner sanctum, to get his friends or acquaintances an audience with the boys.

And Niven Jr was no exception.

But the youngster was persistent as he snuck up beside Alf, and the rest of the entourage headed out to the cars waiting outside.

"Come on, Alf. Get me an autograph. Introduce me, anything," he pleaded.

Alf was stony faced.

"I can't do that. I never do that," he said brushing him aside and somewhat miffed that the teenager had tried to take such a liberty.

He joined the other six in the cars outside, which sped off from the hotel towards the French coast.

The destination was a swanky beachside club, where a table had been booked for the entourage.

"We get in and the waiter put us, as so often happened, in an alcove, for a bit of much-needed privacy.

"Everyone was enjoying this wonderful

French food, when suddenly I heard a commotion."

Alf looked up and grimaced at what he saw. Starstruck Niven Jr, still determined to get an audience with the Fab Four, had pursued them to the exclusive club and had decided on the wacky approach to get their attention.

The youth had, fully clothed, plunged into a fountain in the middle of the restaurant and, to the obvious concern of bemused waiters, was now waving at the band.

"Alf, Alf," he cried out.

Thankfully, attention was diverted from the soaking teenager and Alf was spared the task of explaining his connection.

George had spotted that the club had an adjoining go-kart track. It was closed for the night, with the lights off, but the guitarist, a racing enthusiast, had made his mind up.

The hotel management would normally have been reluctant to allow guests on the track at this late hour – but this was a different story.

"After brief negotiations, we were through by the track, and we all jumped into these go-karts," recalls Alf.

"At first it was complete darkness – then someone decided to switch on the floodlights."

It was too much to resist for paparazzi lurking in bushes in the club grounds, and soon the flashbulbs outshone the floodlights.

"The management noticed all these snappers and quickly turned the lights off again," he said.

There were disastrous consequences for Alf as a result of his lack of vision.

"I went right up the back of George's car, went spinning through the air and came crashing down," he laughs.

"My ankle was in agony. I was taken back to the hotel and a doctor was called.

"It was all strapped up and the doctor said I should fly back to Britain."

But Alf was adamant.

"No way! No way!" he said.

He recalls: "It was pretty badly sprained but I was determined to carry on, albeit with my ankle strapped up."

The Beatles tour made its way to Genoa, with Alf struggling manfully on with his injured ankle. In Italy, however, the chauffeur was himself driven around by some pretty impressive drivers.

"We had four Fiats, each with a member of the Italian racing team taking us about.

"George and I were in one of the cars and, boy, they were good. I thought I was a decent driver but these guys...

"We arrived in Rome and we were staying at the Parque de Princess, which was a beautiful hotel even by Beatle standards. It's all marble."

That night the band, along with Alf, Mal and Neil, headed out to an Italian nightclub.

"As ever, it was glorious. Apart from being with The Beatles, to see these sorts of nightclubs was in itself something wonderful.

"It's not something that a working guy like me could ever in my wildest dreams afford to do.

"But to be there in the company of these legends was quite simply magical."

At 4AM, the boys decided to call it a night. Well, three of them did anyway.

"I ended up with George and this guy, who turned out to be and Italian prince. He offered to show us round Rome," he says.

"So, together with this prince, his beautiful girlfriend and George, I had one of the most wonderful of my times with The Beatles.

"He took us at dawn on this whirlwind tour of Rome. We ended up on some of the Seven Hills of Rome. We were in St Peter's Square and all these wonderful places I'd only seen on picture postcards.

"That was the kind of amazing perk I got when I was with the band."

Later, a less appealing aspect of life on the road with the band was to rear its ugly head – with painful consequences for Alf.

It goes without saying Beatles' security on tour was strict – very strict. There had to be military precision about getting the band from airport to hotel, hotel to gig, back to hotel or nightclub or whatever.

It was all meticulously pre-planned to the last detail. Any discrepancies or glitches in the process could end up in minor, if not fairly serious, disasters. One small but significant example of this was a concert in Rome.

The boys had finished the concert.

As Alf says: "We had an armoured truck. Normally as the last note dies – on 'I'm Down' or whatever they would finish with – we would head off," he says. "There would be an armoured truck – Securicor, or whatever, waiting.

"Neil would lead the way. It always had to be a face that the boys would know to follow. So it was Neil, then John, Paul, George and Ringo and I. Mal would stay behind to deal with the equipment.

"Six of us headed through the stage door into the awaiting armoured truck."

The heavy ranks of security would be told six people would be coming through, and no more. On this occasion an unexpected – an unannounced – seventh figure joined the band.

"Brian Epstein decided to join us. I brought up the rear as number seven."

Security leapt into action as Alf tried to join his colleagues.

"They began beating seven bells out of me because they thought I was an intruder. They didn't know who I was. *Some weirdo is trying to get to the band*, they must have thought."

John and George leapt to his defence, jumping forward shouting: "Leave him alone. Leave him alone – he's one of us."

"All the while these truncheons are whacking down on me. Eventually I got on. I was a bit bruised but my pride was hurt more than anything else."

Next stop Japan. The inaugural flight of Japan Airlines, no less.

"We flew to Tokyo. The Japanese concerts were wonderful," he recalls.

"We flew over the North Pole and by the time we got over North America, there was a problem with the weather, a typhoon or something, so we had to make a landing in Anchorage, which was an experience in itself.

"To spend 15 hours literally on top of the world with The Beatles was somewhat surreal.

"As we made our way to the hotel I noticed they didn't have car parks there but plane parks, with hundreds of bloody Cherokees and so on."

The band whiled away their time in the hotel and Alf befriended a local DJ, who took him down to the docks.

"We were sitting there and he says this is the Baring docks, and 26 miles across there is Siberia and Russia."

Back at the hotel, Alf joined his colleagues at a nightclub at the top of the building, then hit the sack before the first of the Japanese concerts.

The band set up camp in the Tokyo Hilton. In all they were due to play five shows at the legendary Budokan stadium over three days.

"We stayed a few days, and as always the Japanese hospitality was wonderful," he says.

Oriental reaction to the band was in many ways mixed, however.

This was borne out by the demonstrations of Japanese students, who felt the rock and roll playing westerners were a disturbing influence to the young folk.

"In many ways, it was a strange time. Things had started to change the whole Beatles thing," he says.

It was also a time of contemplation within the band. All four had been fond of doodling in an effort to while away the boredom of touring.

On this leg of the tour Alf had noticed the sketches began to take on a darker tone.

Perhaps a legacy of the touring treadmill – although The Beatles' discovery of hallucinogenic substances may have coloured their doodles.

"We set out to play the Budokan, a magnificent venue, and there was a major Japanese student demonstration. Seemingly they were worried that The Beatles would corrupt the young people.

"They thought they would be a bad influence, but it was very much a peaceful protest."

The band arrived at the magnificent Budokan.

"I'd always associated the venue with the martial arts and when we got there, sure enough there were these magnificent statues of samurai warriors above this wonderfully intricate maple floor design."

As the band took to the stage, Alf noticed this wasn't going to be a typical Fab Four gig.

"In the aisles were these imposing looking stewards and every time a fan would jump up as they did the world over, a steward would quickly make them sit down again.

"But the concert was a success and the band were happy."

CHAPTER TEN
The Philippines

IF the band had found the minor student skirmishes of Japan worrying, they were to find a rude awakening on their next visit to the Philippines, easily the scariest time Alf shared with the group in his time as a Beatles employee.

A minor Fab Four aide had made promises to the head of state there, which the group refused to comply with. The results were terrifying. The band arrived in reasonably good spirits and found the usual hysteria at the airport. This however, was commonplace and of no great concern to John, Paul, George and Ringo.

"We were taken to a dockside on Manilla bay and driven out by boat out to this huge yacht in the bay," recalls Alf.

"After a short period, an hour maybe, we asked, 'What's all this about?' and we were told, 'This is where you'll stay during your time in the Philippines'."

The Fab Four were unanimous: "No way!"

Immediately they were all ferried back to the shore and taken to the Manilla Hotel.

"We arrived there and I went to reception to sort out passports and so on. I got the room numbers and as the band were whisked away, I was left to check everyone in.

"There was some old colonial windbag there with medals and so on huffing and puffing that I shouldn't get preferential treatment, but I ignored him and we got checked in."

The first concert – a large outdoor affair – was a success and passed off without incident.

"On the way back to the hotel, I had a feeling of unease, I don't know what but something was up."

Back at their suite in the Hilton, The Beatles relaxed – but not for long.

As was so often the norm, the band, along with their private quarters, had a separate room where they would meet and chat.

As Alf sat watching, someone switched on the television and his earlier fears were confirmed.

"The news came on and said The Beatles were going to attend a reception and banquet with Imelda Marcos – this was certainly news to them," he sighs.

"In no uncertain terms they all said, 'No, this is not going to happen, we're not going to go'.

"Brian was told of their reluctance. He tried to talk them into it, but to no avail."

The band returned from their second show and Alf realised there was something nasty in the air.

"John, Paul, George and Ringo were with Mal in the car in front. I was in a car with a policeman – a plain-clothes guy – and the driver.

"Sitting in the back with me was a guy called Bob Whitaker, the tour photographer. As we drove back we realised there was no doubt about it – all our security had been withdrawn.

"It was a serious blow. The implications for the safety of the band were very serious."

Epstein frantically arranged meetings with Phillipino diplomats, ministers, anyone who could help out in the crisis.

"I became a relay man, taking messages from Brian back to The Beatles and going back to him with their reaction."

It was clear the troubled manager was pinning his hopes on the band caving in and agreeing to meet with Imelda Marcos.

But this wasn't going to happen.

"They were absolutely adamant. There was no way anyone could have persuaded them."

Oddly enough the plain clothes policeman who had been in the car with Alf proved to be a valuable ally in this time of so few friends.

"I remember Bob Whitaker kept having a go at him. Blaming him for the mess we were in and I got really annoyed with this guy who was after all, just a photographer.

"I told him: 'Keep out of this. This is absolutely nothing to do with you. You just stick to taking pictures and let us deal with it'.

"As it turned out, that one plain clothes guy was the only native of Manilla to stand by us. And he fought our corner throughout the nightmare which was to follow."

The Manilla trip was, to everyone's relief, nearly over. Everyone was packed and ready to go to the airport for the flight home.

"Brian had a little travel bag packed. A little British Airways case, which I offered to carry for him. I took it off him, as we headed to the airport."

Manilla Airport was to be the bloody scene of Alf's most traumatic incident with the band.

Philippinos had gathered in their hundreds to wait for the Beatles. Nothing strange in that. It would have been more bizarre if The Fab Four ever left a country without a dramatic send-off.

This was a drama they hadn't bargained for, unfortunately.

The crowds, furious at what they saw as a snub to their beloved leader, Imelda Marcos, were out to avenge the premier.

Alf sighs: "As we headed in, they were on us in an instant. I've been blamed for throwing the first punch.

"George Martin, in particular, has been documented as saying, 'Stupidly, Alf Bicknell raised his fists.'

"I always thought that was pretty rich coming from a guy hundreds of miles away, safely tucked away in a London recording studio.

"Whereas, here I was surrounded by this baying mob, desperate to tear The Beatles to pieces.

"It was my job to protect them. And it was obvious that reasoned arguing wasn't the answer.

"You don't stand there and wait till one of the band is hit. It was a case of 'it's the first blow that counts'."

Soon fists were flying and Alf was surrounded.

"Suddenly someone caught me off-guard with a brutal kick just below the knee. To this day my leg has never really healed from that kick.

"I've had to have several operations."

The blow floored the chauffeur.

"I was annoyed about that because I considered myself, how would you say, a little bit handy. That was part of my job.

"Later when the band were asked about

the Manilla incident, unlike George Martin, they would back me to the hilt. Paul, or whoever, was supportive of my actions and would always give a thumbs-up to the camera, saying, 'Thanks, Alf', as he told reporters I was the only one badly hurt in the fracas.

"What I did, I did to protect them – it was a simple as that. They were in my care."

Bloodied but unbowed, Alf managed to struggle across the concourse and clambered on board the plane with the rest of the entourage.

There was chilly silence as the normally unshakeable Beatles looked out of the window at the mayhem below and tried to come to terms with what had happened.

Eventually a quiet voice spoke up.

"We really could have been – killed out there," whispered Ringo, almost to himself.

Alf adds: "And he was absolutely right."

A few agonising minutes went by and the plane's engines remained ominously quiet. Then the plane intercom crackled into life.

"Would Mr Tony Barrow and Mr Mal Evans please return to the main terminal."

"We looked at each other as if to say,

'What now', but it turned out to be problem with airport taxes, which was quickly resolved.

"The irony of the whole Manilla incident, was that unbeknownst to us, Brian had recorded a message to be broadcast on the news, offering an explanation and apologising for The Beatles' failure to meet with Imelda Marcos.

"Nobody ever saw it. We later learned that come the time for Eppy's message to be broadcast, there was a technical problem. This speech by The Beatles' manager, which was going to explain everything and hopefully placate the rising tension, was never heard.

"The entire television system in the Philippines went down completely just as it was about to be broadcast, which was somewhat bizarre."

Alf describes the period as a somewhat "sweet and sour" situation.

"The tragedy of the Manilla stuff was that it followed the wonderful time we had had in Japan."

The plane stopped at Delhi to drop John, Paul, George and Ringo for their legendary first encounter with the Maharishi.

Alf, Mal, Eppy and the rest of entourage stayed on board.

CHAPTER ELEVEN
The Legend That Was Lennon

DURING his time with The Beatles, Alf developed a close friendship with John Lennon. There were very few occasions when the pair had quarrelled – no mean feat, considering the notoriously mercurial Lennon. And even on these occasions, the fights had been minor and quickly resolved. One occurred while the group were travelling by train, and John was deep in conversation with a journalist a few seats away from Alf. As the chauffeur rose up to stretch his legs, he made eye contact with the singer and smiled at him.

Lennon immediately misinterpreted the grin and, in front of the entire carriage of bemused onlookers he tore into Alf.

"Is something amusing you? D'you find me bloody funny, or something," he stormed.

Alf knew better than to rise to his boss's challenge and the matter was soon forgotten.

Another tiff happened while they were mid-flight in the States.

Alf, John and a couple of others had resorted to their favourite way of passing the time – playing cards.

At one point, Lennon took exception to a remark made by the chauffeur – a comment so innocuous, to this day Alf can't remember what it was – and he lashed out with a tirade of foul-mouthed abuse.

This time Alf was genuinely hurt and not a little angry. Again, however, he thought it better not to argue and headed to the back of the plane.

"The singer Mary Wells was on the tour and I sat opposite her, just sort of thinking."

As he sat staring forlornly out of the window, he heard the clinking of ice and George was above him with two glasses of scotch.

He handed one to Alf and plumped down beside him.

"Don't let it get to you," comforted George. "He really doesn't mean it."

As the plane touched down, Alf gathered up his hand luggage and prepared to get off. At this point, the song "Windmills Of Your Mind" wafted over the plane's speaker system.

It was a particular favourite of Alf's, and he'd told The Beatles how much he loved the track.

On hearing the song, Lennon, who hadn't spoken to him since their row, looked back sheepishly.

He held both hands aloft, grinned at Alf and gave him the thumbs-up, as if to say, "Let's be pals again".

Alf says: "That's the way it was with John, he could flare up very quickly but he was always keen to be mates again."

Lennon had been less than pleased when Alf had used his precious black Rolls Royce to take the group to film an edition of *Blackpool Night Out*, and he thought Alf had caused the car to be damaged.

"John's Rolls had been fitted out with black windows. Actually I think we were one of the first cars in Britain to have black windows.

"I remember looking out for similar windows and never seeing any.

"But it provided a little extra privacy.

Anyway, I asked at the police station in Blackpool if I could use their car park.

"This was fine and I parked it and went to watch the boys record the show. When I went back to pick up the car, I couldn't believe it.

"The windows were all cracked. When I told John he went crazy, he was absolutely raging and thought fans must have got to it.

"I felt awful. I knew he blamed me but there was nothing I could have done. I'd even gone to the bother of parking it behind a police station.

"It actually turned out that the windows had been badly fitted with very little 'give' and had cracked without being touched by anyone."

Trivial as these incidents may seem, they still provide examples of Lennon's mood swings. At other times, Alf was on the receiving end of Lennon's savage wit, which many found too cruel.

On one such occasion, the chauffeur was taking the boys and their equipment to a TV show.

He had strapped two guitars, which the band jokingly referred to as banjos, to the boot of the car.

As they drove along, the chauffeur noticed a lorry was tailing him and the driver seemed to be signalling furiously for him to stop.

Somewhat flustered, Alf pulled onto the hard shoulder.

The driver told him one of the guitars had fallen off the back of the vehicle.

Alf thanked him and made his way slowly to the back door of the Princess.

He nervously explained to Lennon, who was nearest: "I think, erm, we've lost one of the banjos."

Fixing him with an icy stare, Lennon shot back: "Really. Well, I'll tell you what, Alf. Find that banjo and you'll get a bonus."

Curiosity got the better of the driver and he asked: "Really. What sort of bonus, John?"

John said coolly: "You get to keep your job."

Now panicking and fearing the worst, Alf re-traced his route – and his worst fears were confirmed. The guitar was smashed in bits, lying all across the road.

Fortunately Lennon was kidding and

their friendship continued.

"Mainly what I remember about John was the laughter. He had a very bizarre but infectious sense of humour.

"He had me fit speakers – underneath his car.

"And he had all these real-life recordings on an eight-track. Explosions and so on.

"So we'd be driving down Regent Street at like three in the morning and as we passed different groups of people, John would pop on one of these tapes.

"Suddenly there would be the deafening sound of a plane taking off or a train speeding through a tunnel at 90 miles an hour.

"People didn't know what the heck was going on, they'd be looking round for this plane or a train. They were so freaked, and John would be in stitches."

On another occasion Alf was taking John and George to a club. Lennon had once more entrusted him with the Rolls.

"It was all mod cons this car. Apart from the black windows, it was kitted out with all the latest hi-tech gear, including a state-of-the-art telly in the back.

"I'd just picked up George from Claremont Estate and he was nattering away to John. They were sort of oblivious to the telly, which was showing a programme called *Codename*, a detective series starring Ian Hendry.

"We were travelling along the A3, coming from St George's Hill, Claremont Estate in Esher up towards North London, Montague Square by Baker Street.

"I noticed in the rear-view mirror we were being tailed by this car, a Jaguar. I was doing around 90 or 95 mph. The A3 was dual carriageway but there were some stretches which were single track road.

"As we approached Kensington, just touching Olympia, John suddenly shouted, 'That's us!'

"It turned out the car behind us was a police car. They were using the police radio and talking about the Rolls in front of them, which they thought was stolen."

The TV aerial in John's car was picking up the police message and giving John and

George a detailed commentary of Alf's route: "Kensington Street – they are now turning into the Bayswater Road, Sussex Gardens."

Alf recalls: "I pulled into Montague Mews, which was a dead end, and stopped the Rolls. The Jaguar had parked at the top of the street and a young policeman had got out and was walking towards us.

"I jumped out of the car and realised I was dressed casually, no chauffeur's uniform, just jeans and a t-shirt."

The officer eyed the blacked out car and said: "Good evening, Sir. Can I have a look in the car?"

Alf shot back indignantly: "What for?" then said reluctantly, "OK, but you open the door."

The policeman carefully pulled the back door open to see Lennon and Harrison curled up laughing in the back seat.

Gobsmacked he turned to Alf: "You... you were doing nearly 100mph back there."

The driver shot back: "Listen mate, I didn't know who the hell you were. You see who I'm driving? D'you blame me for putting the foot down when I think there's someone dodgy following us?"

The still-reeling officer replied, "I guess not," and headed off into the night.

One Saturday morning – a rare day off – Alf was preparing his fishing rods for a relaxed day by the riverside. No such luck.

The phone rang. It was John.

"What you doing, Alf?" he said.

Alf gazed forlornly at his fishing gear, before replying: "Well, it looks like I'll be coming round to see you."

He jumped into the Austin Princess and headed round to John's house.

The door was open when he got there.

Alf, who by this stage was completely relaxed around his world-famous bosses, wandered in.

"Hello, it's me," he shouted.

No reply.

He eventually found the singer in the dining room surrounded by toast and a freshly brewed pot of coffee.

"Hi, Alf have a seat," he said.

The pair sat together munching toast,

sipping coffee, smoking cigarettes and idly chatting.

Eventually Alf, remembering his cancelled fishing trip, asked: "Well, what are we going to do, then?"

"Come with me," said John.

They wandered out of the dining room up a flight of stairs and along one of the long winding corridors in John's house to a room right at the far side of the building.

The room was bare, no furniture, no curtains – just one solitary bare light bulb in the centre.

John stepped inside of this large imposing bare room and announced: "We, me and you, are going to decorate this entire room. We're going to make it great."

"Right," replied Alf. "You do have the stuff?"

"No, that's your first job. You've to go and get that."

Heading back out of the room Alf made a mental note of what he'd need for the job. Brushes, palettes, and paint.

"What colour paint, John?"

The singer looked round the room, stroked his chin before saying decisively: "Red, Alf. Pillar box red."

Off he went to the DIY store and piled all the stuff into the back of the Austin Princess.

Alf recalls: "So I spent the next two weeks at John's doing up this room with him. There was more paint on the floor than on the walls by the time we finished.

"In between the decorating we'd go into an adjoining room which had a giant Scalextric track with like eight lanes. He had little Mini Coopers and Lotus Elans and we would have these crazy races against each other.

"When we were fed up with that we would do a bit more painting, or if were bored doing that we would head down to the lounge where John had this very grand electric organ.

"He had a sort of machine next to it, which had like sax or clarinet or whatever sound you wanted from the organ. So John would start playing and shout out to me what instrument he'd like and I'd press all these buttons."

Alf saw a side of the legend that was Lennon, which he feels is so often forgotten.

"There was a side to him that was soft and gentle," he says.

"There was a sort of magic around him. He was quite simply great to be around, great to be with."

CHAPTER TWELVE
McCartney

THE phone rang and a familiar voiced inquired of Alf: "What you up to?" It was early morning and Alf was getting dressed, when he'd taken the call. "Not much, what's up?" the chauffeur answered, wearily rubbing his tired eyes. Paul McCartney answered with a further question: "You had breakfast? No? Come round, then." At this time the Beatle was staying at a flat in the home of his then girlfriend, Jane Asher. It was an invitation Alf found hard to resist, he knew the sort of spread which would await him when he arrived.

"Jane Asher's mum did the best cooked breakfast around – terrific. She was particularly good at fried tomatoes, they were always just right. I've never met anybody who could do the tomatoes like she used to do them," Alf drools at the memory.

"We sat at the kitchen, munching and

chatting. I always felt at ease, very relaxed around Paul. He finished his breakfast long before me and headed out of the room.

"I could tell he was up to something.

"So I'm sitting there drinking my coffee and finishing my toast – Mrs Asher's fried tomatoes now just a memory.

"Suddenly this figure appears in the doorway.

"I spat out a mouthful of coffee. Before me was a real sight to behold."

The ever-resourceful Macca had prepared one of his famous 'disguises' for the shopping trip he intended taking with his chauffeur.

"It was so funny to me. He had this long overcoat on. This bizarre-looking false moustache and these tortoiseshell glasses on and hat roughly pulled down over his forehead.

"I'd seen loads of his disguises and I never let on if I thought they looked silly. I always tried to keep a straight face."

Paul announced: "We're going shopping – for a grandfather clock."

They scoured the London streets – Harrow Road, Portobello Market – Alf at the wheel. Occasionally Paul would spot an antiques shop and they'd dive out to have a look.

"It was hilarious; there's me with Paul in this ridiculous get-up. And just about everyone in the shops recognised him and I could see them quietly chuckling to themselves.

"But Paul was oblivious. I really think he believed he'd cracked the anonymity bit."

It was the same story in each of the stores, with the owners pretending they didn't realise they had Macca on their premises.

As lunchtime approached and decent grandfather clocks were proving to be an elusive commodity, the pair decided to retire to the bar.

"We still hadn't found this bloody clock, so we went for a drink in Ladbroke Road.

"I ordered a couple of pints and straightaway, I clocked the bar staff checking out Paul and clearly recognising him.

"And he's there in the background triumphantly dabbing back this ridiculous peeling-off moustache, thinking he's blending in with the crowd. People started coming up to me, 'Is that Paul McCartney?' and so on.

"I sat down with him and advised him to

drink up quickly."

A bemused Paul patted his false moustache, drained the last of his pint and the pair left.

McCartney's easy-going nature seemed to stretch back to his family, who Alf had the pleasure of staying with.

"He'd phoned me and asked if I'd take him up to Liverpool. We drove up to his father, who lived on the Wirral."

As ever, the trusty Austin Princess would be used. On these informal trips, the Beatle Alf was driving around would sit up front with the chauffeur for a natter.

This occasion was no different, with Paul in particularly good spirits, the way he always was on visits to his home town.

When they arrived at the house in the Wirral, Paul's father was there to greet them. He embraced his son and then turned to the driver.

"Come on, Alf, let's go for a drink."

Alf laughs: "So me and Paul's dad headed off to the pub and probably had a few too many beers. His dad was a wonderful person. I only met him a few times. But there was a great spiritual feeling about him – you immediately trusted him, when you met him.

"Anyway, we chatted and laughed over our drinks. He was obviously very proud of his pop star son and seemed to appreciate the various stories I could tell him about the band.

"This I think was on a Thursday and I was staying at his dad's house. We got back quite late and I headed off to bed."

The next couple of days saw Paul and Alf relaxing over some wonderful home cooking.

On the Saturday, some of Paul's relatives were due to visit and Alf, ever aware that he should let the McCartney clan have a bit of space, decided to stay in his room.

"It was big party, which had been planned for that night. I stayed out of the way for a bit.

"I flicked through a few magazines and must have dozed off."

Some time later, he was awoken by the sound of a piano and singing.

It was mid-evening, and most of the guests had arrived. Alf decided it would be OK to head down.

"I get down and there's all these people – there must have been between 50 and 60 McCartneys – all gathered there."

In the middle of the throng was their most famous son, holding court.

"Paul was sat at the piano, playing all these old music hall numbers. All really old classics like 'Old Mother Kelly's Doorstep', going right back to the old war songs.

"No Beatles songs, just standards. And all his relatives were singing along – it was so touching, I'll never forget it."

Paul ran through a number of traditional songs, picking out the chords and leading the rest of the singers.

After a while he stopped, resisting the requests pouring in from his aunts and uncles.

"He spotted me and introduced me to all these people.

"It was clear he saw me as a friend, rather than an employee, as I shook hands with his various relatives.

"I was genuinely touched by that."

And Alf's feeling that The Beatles' feet were always on the ground was again borne out.

"He was so relaxed. No showbiz nonsense, he was just one of the family. Not affected by his fame or fortune."

CHAPTER THIRTEEN
Ringo

IF John and Paul were the main creative force behind the band, and George the spiritual character, it was Ringo with his down-to-earth approach and complete lack of airs and graces, who was the man Alf felt in many ways kept them together through the madness.

"He was the joker and – I mean this positively – a very homely individual," he recalls. "A very caring person. I remember I would take him up to Liverpool to see his mum, Elsie. She was a lovely lady who would always make me extremely welcome. He had a stepfather, Harry, and they were such great people."

On one particularly memorable occasion Alf had the pleasure of ferrying the Starkey family around London. Like Alf himself, Ringo's stepdad was a Londoner, from the East Side.

"So naturally we head off for the East

Side of the Capital, there's me driving, Harry and Elsie and Ringo himself. I think at the time Harry and Elsie were in their late 70s, early 80s. It was a magical family gathering as we cruised down the east London streets, with Harry reminiscing about his childhood, pointing out his old schools, favourite cafes and so on. Ringo very much took a back seat and let his stepdad hold court. There was a really convivial atmosphere and a sense of the family's closeness.

"Occasionally Ringo would be spotted, but he was in good spirits and we'd stop so he could chat to Beatles fans, or sign autographs."

Alf was to play a crucial part in the wedding of Ringo and Maureen, an occasion when, again, he got to know the drummer's family very closely. As ever, preparation was the key to ensure much-needed privacy on the big day.

"It was all kept a closely-guarded secret. 24 hours before the wedding we went to a secret address in Chelsea, this grand house in the Kings Road where Ringo and Maureen and the various in-laws could unwind," says Alf. "With all the mayhem surrounding the group, I always tried to ensure they had their own space as much as possible, though obviously it wasn't very easy.

"At this address in Chelsea, we had complete privacy. There was Ringo's mum and stepdad, Maureen's folks and a few others. There was obviously great excitement about the next day's wedding, Maureen's mum in particular could hardly contain her joy at having Ringo as a son-in-law. She could hardly sit down for a second, nattering on ten to the dozen to anyone who would listen about the wedding."

The wedding party stayed there overnight, and Alf passed away Ringo's last few hours of bachelordom in typical Beatles style – out came the card set.

"As ever, I ended up skint. By this time Ringo was one hell of a card player. We usually played 'put and take', a sort of game of chance, and he would fleece me at that most of the time. Still, it was worth it to see him so relaxed. We reminisced for a while and then Ringo asked me if I would do him a favour. He wanted me to take the bride and groom's parents out for a good old knees-up after the wedding was over.

Of course, I was very honoured he entrusted his future in-laws with me. The wedding at Caxton Hall went smoothly and Ringo and Maureen headed off on honeymoon to the south coast of England."

Alf and another driver, who was in Brian Epstein's employ and was used on the day, had to keep the in-laws happy for the night for a grand wedding party without the bride and groom.

"Myself and this guy tossed to see who would drive and I won, so it meant I could have a few beers and let my hair down with these folk. We took them to the East End of London for a swanky dinner followed by a singsong. The East End at the time had these wonderful talent shows every night of the week, so we had plenty of places to go. We went from pub to pub and it was a wonderful way to celebrate the wedding we'd just been to. I did get a bit tipsy, but then I didn't have to worry about driving. It was one of the few occasions where I could have a few beverages and really muck in. I remember many toasts to Ringo and his new bride that night."

A close bond had been built up between

Alf and the drummer, when the band went to tour Australia and Ringo was forced to stay behind due to ill-health. At this stage the chauffeur wasn't well established enough to be invited on the Antipodean tour and besides, as he says himself:

"Someone had to stay behind and look after Ringo. I took Ringo into University College Hospital, where he was to have an operation on his tonsils, remembers Alf. After the operation, I arrived to take him back to King Williams Mews, where he was staying, although he later moved to Montague Square. As always, a crowd of fans had gathered but I managed to usher him through the throng into the car without too much fuss."

When Ringo made the move to his new home in Montague Square, Alf's wife developed a close bond with the late Maureen Starkey. Alf had to take the drummer to hospital on another occasion, this time when his wife Maureen went into labour. The driver has never been more grateful for the trusty suspension of the Austin Princess. He'll never forget the phone call at 2AM from a distraught Ringo at his Mews flat:

"Alf, can you come at once. I think Maureen's having the baby."

He recalls: "I probably lived only about five minutes away, so I'm round there in minutes, no time at all. The fact it was at that time in the morning was definitely a bonus, because we had to go right across town to get to the maternity ward. Montague Square was in the Edgware Road area, and we had to get him down to the other side of Chiswick, which was about five miles. We sped on down right through Bayswater Road, right the way through Shepherds Bush, with both Ringo and I praying she wouldn't have the baby till we got there. I'll never forget Ringo and Maureen in the back of the Princess. Every little bump in the road, every slight swerve and it was "Ohhhhhh" from Maureen. Me and Ringo were praying she'd hang on until we got there. Mercifully we eventually arrived at Queen Charlottes hospital, where she had the baby a few hours later. There were so overjoyed with little Zak – who some say is a better drummer than his father – and I was so glad to have been there to help."

Alf has many enduring images of his

days helping ferry the drummer around. One memorable occasion was at John's house.

"It's obviously well-documented that John and Paul would always create a track for Ringo to record for each album. And the time had come to pick a suitable song for the *Help!* album. We were sat round John's big dining room table; there was John at the head of the table, Ringo sitting opposite. They were trying out all sorts of ideas, John strumming away on the guitar, but nothing he and Paul had come up with seemed to gel. Then Lennon had a brainwave.

"'Buck Owen and the Buckaroos, that would be perfect,' he said and began strumming the chords to 'Act Naturally'. Ringo was a bit perplexed at first but soon he had perked up and was singing along with John. So it was great to be there and watch them trade ideas off each other, and then to see this idea being born. It was actually one of the few times I was with them when there was this sense of collaboration. They actually sat there and worked out between them what they were going to do."

CHAPTER FOURTEEN
George

THE day after Christmas, 1965, Alf received a call from George Harrison, who wanted to go and visit his family back in Liverpool.

"I'd had Christmas Day off – it was rare to be off at all. But I didn't mind it, was such an honour and a privilege to be around them. In this whirlwind, this hurricane, which was to change so much."

He duly drove the guitarist up, and as ever, discovered The Beatles' families were gracious hosts and welcomed the stranger as one of their own.

"They were all delighted to see George, of course, but they went out of their way to make sure I felt welcome and comfortable in the house. I stayed with his mum and dad and brothers and sisters and so on. There was a bedroom in their loft, I remember, and I slept there. George was in a bed over on the other side of the loft.

I remember we had to pull down these steps in the kitchen to get to this huge great area above, which had been converted.

They were all so unaffected, The Beatles and their families. That's what really struck me. Even with all this amazing music they were making, which would be remembered for so long, they were still so down-to-earth – and that is what really endeared them to me.

Alf spent a few days getting to know George's Liverpool, with the pair visiting the youngest Beatle's old haunts.

"On the night we arrived he took me out, and it wasn't to some swanky restaurant or glitzy club. It was places like the Legion, real sort of working men's clubs."

And there were no pretensions about the guitarist as he met up with old school friends and their families and so on.

"George would introduce me to his friends and family. Not by saying 'This is our driver' but, 'This is Alf'.

"Whoever met me would shake my hand and welcome me warmly. That camaraderie that existed in Liverpool was amazing.

"Soon our table was surrounded by well-wishers and the drink would be flowing."

It wasn't until the early hours that the pair would stagger back to George's house.

It usually took several attempts before the pair had precariously climbed up the telescope ladders in the kitchen, all the while Alf giggling and shooshing Harrison in a vain attempt to keep the noise down.

"In the loft, George was in this small cot-type bed and I'm at the other end, up in the roof on this makeshift bed. I have very fond memories of that time.

"We were both usually a bit tired and the worse for drink but we still had a natter about how things had changed for George since the Fab Four had hit the big time.

"We chatted about the pressures of fame and so on and then before I realised it, I would have fallen asleep and the next thing it would be morning in the Harrison household."

The pressures of fame the pair discussed included the obvious things, like not being able to shop for clothes without being mobbed –

particularly frustrating for the style-icon Fab Four.

George also revealed he missed heading out to the pictures.

Occasionally it would be engineered, with customary military precision, that the boys could visit a cinema in London. This usually involved carefully liaising with the management, who would let the boys slip in the second the lights had gone down. But trying to enjoy the latest release, knowing you could be spotted any second and would probably have to make a sharp exit, was not the ideal way to relax at the flicks.

So Alf and George hit on the concept of home cinema.

"It turned out a company called Seamans were producing a great 16 millimetre projector at this time.

"By the time I tracked down a place that sold them in London, the rest of the band had decided home cinema was the way for them to enjoy new releases too.

"So of course when they guy in the shop asks me if I want a Seamans projector, it wasn't just George I was shopping for. 'I'll have four please,' I said.

"So now you have all four Beatles with these projectors set up in their various houses, but they all need films.

"So off I head down to Columbia, Paramount, 20th Century Fox, United Artists and so on, to pick up the latest releases. Mind you, when they heard where their films were going, the film companies were always happy to oblige."

It was just another little thing that meant The Beatles – particularly intensely private people like George – could feel less of a prisoner in their own homes. They could sit with their families and watch a new movie like any other family. But the main thing is they'd be safe, without any hassle from fans.

It wasn't just George's home cinema brainwave which had to be multiplied four-fold but, usually, anything one of the band came up with.

"I'd hear, 'Can you get me a couple of cashmere sweaters, Alf?' and then, 'Yeah, me too', 'Me too', and 'Me too'. So off I'd go down to one of the big stores in London and it would be, 'Cashmere sweaters please. Two beige, two brown, two black, two of this, two of that', and so on.

"I'd usually throw in a couple for myself, too. I'd never pay for them. A note would be made of what I'd taken and it would be squared up later."

The requests would range from the practical suits, shoes and so on, to the downright bizarre.

"On one occasion, George asked me if I could lay my hands on a gorilla suit, of all things. They all used to love to lark about. obviously, and I suppose this was a natural progression.

"So I ended up finding a guy who was prepared to make me gorilla outfits. This was in the West End of London, Kensington High Street. I think he was a fancy dress hire and retail shop, and sure enough he ended up making me four of these giant hairy suits."

As it turned out, this particular whim was very short-lived and The Beatles never even bothered seeing the suits.

"They ended up in a cupboard in my

house and my son and his mates had a great time clowning around in these ape outfits."

CHAPTER FIFTEEN
Brian Epstein

THE Beatles were in the middle of a European tour. Fresh from playing one concert in Nice, the band flew onto Madrid. This was the start of July, 1965, and the group were scheduled to play the famous Plaza de Toros de Las Ventas bullring. As the boys relaxed in the communal dressing room, Brian Epstein came in, looking very excited and clutching a pair of tickets.

Eppy had got his hands on ringside seats for a bullfight that day, but he needed someone to accompany him to this bloody spectacle.

Slowly he worked his way round the band, imploring each one in turn to watch the dashing Spanish matadors in action. But the reaction from John, Paul, George and Ringo was the same.

Lennon summed up the view of the rest of the band: "No way Brian. I wouldn't be seen dead at a bullfight."

The manager looked downcast for a second, then his eyes made contact with Alf, and he said: "How about you, Alf? Come on, they're the best seats in the house."

The chauffeur couldn't think of anywhere he'd less like to be, but realised this was his boss who was making the request, and as ever he went along with him.

"Suddenly, I'm in the back of this limo with Brian, heading through the streets of Madrid to see this bullfight. But it wasn't really a case of being intimidated.

"He was always very charming and courteous. There was never any bigshot music business thing with Eppy.

"He was very serious about the band, obviously, but he never belittled anyone."

Alf found the spectacle of the bullfight a little harder to stomach, as they sat watching from their ringside seats.

Epstein, however, became very animated at the bloody spectacle.

"He seemed to love the whole thing. The matadors and the bulls. It was actually one time when he really seemed to let go of the conservative, cool image he was renowned for.

"I was sitting there trying to miss the bloodier moments and Brian was cheering on the proceedings.

"I didn't say anything. I sort of went along with it – probably because no one else would."

The other times Brian would let his hair down were when he would join in the regular card games the band and their entourage would take part in.

"When Brian was involved there were usually very high stakes. Sometimes £500 at the turn of a card – a lot of money in those days.

"I can still see him in Benedict Canyon, where we were staying, almost beside himself with excitement as he gambled away these huge sums of cash."

The manager's homosexuality was never an issue. It was something never spoken about during Alf's employ.

The only time it was alluded to was during the tour of Japan.

"We were staying at the Tokyo Hilton and it just happened that Brian and I ended up in this large suite of rooms together – just the two of us.

"Brian seemed nervous at first, and then said he wanted to ask my advice about something.

"He looked away for a second, obviously choosing his words and said, 'Alf, I have someone working for me and I'm a bit worried'.

"You see the thing is they know a lot about me – an awful lot about my private business and I'm a little concerned."

Alf quickly realised what his boss was hinting at and replied: "It's simple, Brian. Just bloody sack him. Immediately."

"About a year after I left, he died. Another of the terrible tragedies that surrounded the band.

"John, Maureen Starkey, Mal Evans and even people in the background like Wendy Hanson, who was Brain's personal assistant.

"She died after tripping down a flight of stairs in Italy. Latterly, of course, there was Linda McCartney. So much heartache around the band."

Alf remembers Brian with great

fondness.

"What always struck me about him was his great devotion to The Beatles, coupled with a deliberate lack of interference.

"He took everything as it was – this small unit of people making this amazing music. Everyone worked and gelled together and that suited Brian fine.

"With concerts or in the studio, Brian just let the boys get on with it."

Alf was aware of the manager's hunger to do something outside the band.

"He always had a hankering to be an actor. That's partly the reason he took over the lease of the Saville Theatre.

"I think he'd have loved to have been on the stage. But my lasting impression of Brian will be of him at The Beatles shows. There, resplendent in his suit and ever-present polka-dot scarf, he'd watch intently from the wings like a proud parent.

"He seemed to be trying to drink in the atmosphere, as he listened to the screams as his four boys took to the stage.

"That's when Brian was at his happiest."

CHAPTER SIXTEEN
Hamburg

THE Fab four's "trio in waiting", Neil, Mal and Alf, would always keep a watchful eye out for their charges. Nowhere was this more prevalent than in the dressing rooms before and after shows. There was one occasion, however, when the all three decided that for once they should step back and let John, Paul, George and Ringo vet their own visitors – on their triumphant return to Hamburg on June 26, 1966.

As the Beatles' train pulled into the station, Alf sensed there was magic in the air.

"The train we used on that leg of the tour was amazing, even by Beatle standards.

"It was used by the Queen when she visited Germany and was palatial indeed. We lived like royalty. Each of us, the boys, Brian, Neil, Tony, Mal and I had our own suites on board.

"We'd all meet up for meals or a game

of cards, though the band spent a lot of time catching up with their sleep as the train moved through Germany."

The entourage had pulled into Hamburg very early in the morning, about 6AM.

Alf had managed to enjoy a quick breakfast with George, just cereal and some coffee.

"It's weird, Alf," said George, eyeing up a spoonful of cornflakes. "Last time we were in Hamburg we were living on these."

It was here in Hamburg, of course, three years before that they honed their craft and developed a following so many miles from Liverpool. The band hadn't set foot there since.

Now it was a different story. They had returned to their adopted home as heroes – the biggest band on the planet – and Alf sensed there was something special in the air.

It was a Sunday and the group were scheduled to play two shows at the Ernst Merck Halle.

Old faces began to arrive to congratulate the band they'd watched in a tiny Hamburg club just months ago.

The Beatles hadn't forgotten, and tears and laughter filled the air as they greeted staff from the Star Club where they had had a residency, and old friends like Astrid Kirchherr and Bert Kaempfert.

"There's a classic photo of myself, Neil and Mal, uncharacteristically slouching back on these chairs in the dressing room in Hamburg," says Alf.

"We were watching this procession of friends of the band who had all become close to the boys before they became famous.

"It was so moving. Normally, we'd be keeping an eye out to see who was coming in, but on this occasion we realised the best thing would be to stay out of it.

"We didn't even listen or take heed of who came through. It was a private moment of reunion for the band to meet their old pals."

It was certainly a far cry from some of the other venues, when record company lackeys, their wives' friends and so on would come to press the flesh.

Innocent as this may seem, Alf became alarmed when he realised children were being used in the equation.

"There was a time – at places like the Hammersmith Odeon – when people used to bring their children, however young, along to see the band," he recalls.

"Some were very obviously backward children and these youngsters would be taken along to the dressing room and there was something unwholesome about it. It was always a little difficult.

"You had these people with poor unfortunate kids and they'd present them to Paul and John and there was definitely an awkwardness there. It was clear that the parents were the benefactors in this situation, and sort of using their young ones to find a legitimate reason to meet the band.

"I think John particularly used to get embarrassed by it."

But there were no such reservations backstage in Hamburg. The shows themselves were emotional affairs. As Alf watched from the wings he sensed a renewed vigour as the Fab Four put a little extra into their performance as they played two energetic sets in front of crowds of nearly 6,000.

Emotions were clearly running high for a lot of people that night. The fans' hysteria had reached fever pitch and more than 40 Hamburg youths were arrested by police for rioting both inside and outside of the Ernst Merck Halle.

"Despite the obvious presence of some dangerously unruly fans, I remember John and Paul decided to sneak along to the Rieperbahn later that night.

"John told me later he'd almost been in tears as they strolled past some of their old Hamburg haunts, popping in occasionally to cafés and bars to see if familiar faces from the early days were still around.

"But time had moved on, he told me, for The Beatles. And as John discovered that night, time had also moved on for their old pals in Hamburg."

CHAPTER SEVENTEEN
Bigger Than Jesus

THE furore surrounding John Lennon's assertion that his band were "more popular than Jesus" is well-documented and marks, with the mayhem in Manilla, a dark chapter in The Beatles' career.

Originally, John's views on Christianity had come buried deep towards the end of an interview in the *London Evening Standard*. The piece had passed relatively unnoticed. However, nothing could prepare the Fab Four for the reaction Stateside, more than five months after the original article.

An American teen magazine had lifted the article and by employing the old tabloid favourite of taking quotes out of context had come up with the front page splash headline: "John Lennon: I don't know which will go first – Christianity, or rock and roll."

There then followed the complete banning of the group's music on dozens of radio stations and the infamous Beatles bonfires.

Enraged DJs urged teenage fans to collect all their Fab Four paraphernalia, records, posters and so on, and torch them in a public display of revulsion at Lennon's words.

The enormous gravity of the situation wasn't lost on Alf, or indeed Epstein.

As fires were lit up across America and the burning hatred of the Beatles by bible-bashing fanatics became apparent, their beleaguered manager seriously considered pulling the tour.

Epstein was more fearful than ever that one of his boys might be shot.

However, after a hastily arranged press conference, where John "apologised" for his remark, it was agreed the tour would go on.

But the Jesus issue dogged all the subsequent press conferences.

"In interview after interview John would say, 'How many times do I have to say I'm sorry'," recalls Alf.

It was clear Lennon's patience was wearing thin.

"He was getting really fed up facing the

same subject at every press conference."

At the time the band was travelling with an entourage of about a dozen journalists.

But it was the local hacks who were fanning the flames of controversy.

"Kenny Everett was with us. Don Shaw of the *Daily Mirror*, various American magazine writers and newspaper men, together with disc jockeys.

"But it was the local Press in each of the cities we arrived in who would cause the trouble."

The most disturbing element, where the feelings of the fanatics became all too apparent, came on August 19 in Memphis, when the band were scheduled to play two shows.

The group sat in the communal hotel room chatting, a TV flickered in the background.

Suddenly a news item came on which sent a chill down Alf's spine.

"They were interviewing this guy, dressed up in the full Ku Klux Klan rig-out. The white robes and the giant pointed hood.

"He was basically promising to have The Beatles assassinated, saying 'Somehow we will get them and we will kill them'."

With these chilling words still ringing in their ears, The Beatles set out for the first of their shows at the Coliseum in Memphis. The band's giant dressing room was matched by the venue's magnificent stature.

As the group filed in with Brian, Alf, Mal and Neil, they stopped to admire the breathtaking centrepiece, a long refectory-style table laden with every kind of food imaginable; succulent-looking fresh fruit, giant cheeses and fine wines. Thankfully the band still had a few friends left, as these wonderful gifts from fans testified.

"We were stood there looking at this delicious-looking spread, almost transfixed, when there was a knock on the door. Mal answered it and standing there was this very serious-looking Police Captain."

Without greeting the band the officer walked in and said: "I don't want to alarm you boys, but we have a problem. We've received information to say that there is a bomb under the stage."

Hardly missing a beat, Lennon moved

towards the table of food shouting back at Alf: "Alf, go and sort it out."

It seems the band thought that as well as his fighting skills, and experience as a drugs courier, the chauffeur had another string to his bow – as a crack bomb disposal expert.

Dutifully Alf headed off towards the stage, more worried about getting his favourite light grey suit dirty than anything else.

He searched high and low around the backs of curtains, behind amps, then finally he clambered under the stage for a thorough look.

"I hadn't realised how big and complex these stages were. There I was going in and out of all these girders.

"There was nothing there, so I headed back, filthy from climbing under this dusty old stage."

Alf's intentions of tucking into some of the delicious backstage food were dashed as soon as he opened the dressing room door.

"Everybody had had their fill while I was away. The table had been massacred.

"As usual, people were lying around on chairs and what they called cots. John was tuning a guitar but looked up and said, 'Hi Alf'.

"Despite the fact I hadn't found anything, there was still tension in the air."

It was during the second show that the fear reached fever pitch.

"They went on as usual. It was the standard line-up, as I looked from the auditorium – John, Ringo, George and Paul.

"Again, I tried to stand out of camera shot as it were – I guess I was closest to John.

"They were playing away when suddenly there was a loud bang. Everyone jumped. Of course our first thought was that a gun had been fired.

"We were all looking round to see who had been shot. It turned out someone had let off firework in the audience."

Happily, the show passed off without further incident, and Elvis fanatic Mal Evans received an open invitation to visit Graceland.

CHAPTER EIGHTEEN
America, 1966: The Final Curtain

CANDLESTICK Park in San Francisco. Here on
Monday, August 29, 1966, 25,000 fans would
witness The Beatles' final concert. It was a time
of mixed feelings for all concerned. The band
were tired – and had been for a long time – of
playing to audiences who seemed oblivious to
the music and intent on drowning the woefully
inadequate PAs with their ear-splitting screams.

On this rainy windswept night, there was
a chill in the air as the group took to the stage.
John and Paul each carried cameras and would
take quick snaps of themselves and the audience
between songs. They knew they were
documenting the end of an era. After an
energetic set lasting just over half an hour, the
last chords of "Long Tall Sally" rang out and
The Fab Four left the stage – forever.

"They bounded into the dressing room
and John plonked himself down next to me. I

could tell there was something on his mind," recalls Alf.

"'That's it,' he announced, almost triumphantly. 'No more touring.'"

There was a hushed silence and then a few seconds later another voice made a proclamation; "That's it – I'm no longer a Beatle."

It was George. Then, finally a third voice piped up.

"That's it for me, as well."

This time, Alf had spoken.

"It had been two years. A magical time, with me privy to one of the most exciting times in the last century."

Paul turned to Alf and patted him on the back, saying: "I understand, Alf. We'll never forget you. You were with us in the eye of the hurricane."

Alf recalls: "I'd been privileged to be along for the ride. But like the band, the repetition had sort of got to me.

"For them it was an endless parade of limousines, hotels, dressing rooms, frenetic concerts, more dressing rooms, more hotels, more limousines – and on and on it went.

"To me there was something unproductive about the whole touring process. They just weren't creating."

EPILOGUE
The End Of A
Long And Winding Road

THOUGH he was offered, not surprisingly, a number of chauffeuring jobs by various rock stars after handing in his notice to the Fab Four, Alf declined them all. As he says today, "How can you top The Beatles? It's impossible." Instead he undertook a number of low-key jobs, ferrying various "captains of industry" to high-powered meetings, and even a lengthy spell driving wine connoisseurs around some of France's vineyards.

"That was glorious, but so far removed from my work with John, Paul, George and Ringo.

"Instead of being pursued by an army of crazed fans, I would leisurely take these wine tasters up and down the south of France, dropping in on various vineyards on the way," he says.

Another lengthy spell was spent in the employ of a wealthy Norwegian businessman.

"That was in a Phantom 5, the same car John used to drive."

But that was the only reference point he had to his time with the band.

He never spoke about The Beatles to his new employers and would only occasionally regale his friends with tales of his days at the heart of Beatlemania – after "one glass of wine too many".

Only on one occasion in the intervening years did he have any kind of re-union with his former bosses – and that was purely by chance.

"This would have been in 1976, when I was staying in Reading. I came out of my front door and who should pull out of a side street in his Porsche, but George Harrison," says Alf.

"He immediately stopped and jumped out. We gave each other a hug and chatted about all the old days.

"I remembered we started arguing in a friendly way about the night I visited Bob Dylan in London. George insisted I wasn't there, and we just couldn't agree.

"Eventually, we decided we'd maybe gone on different nights. Anyway, we embraced again and George drove off."

Less pleasant, however, was the news of the death of another old Beatles buddy in a horrific shooting incident in the States.

"I was sat in the Rolls in London's Berkeley Square, when this announcement came on about Mal Evans being shot dead," he says.

"That was so devastating. He'd moved to the West Coast of America to make a new start, but it all went horribly wrong."

Even more shocking news was to follow.

After a grim chainsaw accident, Alf was laid up in bed. The incident would leave him partially paralysed in one arm.

As he lay semi-sleeping, his body pumped up with pain killers, his son ran into the room.

"He's dead, Dad. John's been murdered," said Mark.

Still dazed, Alf couldn't quite come to terms with Lennon's assassination. His eyes welling up with tears, he turned and gazed out of his bedroom window.

"We had some conifer trees in the garden and I just stared at them for what seemed like hours. So many memories ran through my head.

"John pulling the cap from me and telling me I was now 'one of them', a Beatle. Playing Scalextric with him.

"So many images. From him singing his heart out on stage – to him sitting at his dining table munching toast and sipping a mug of coffee, as he read the morning papers.

"And now he was gone. I would never speak to him or see him again. This madman had taken him away from us.

"As these thoughts filtered through my mind, I kept looking at the conifers. Ever since then, trees have always reminded me of John."

Some years later in 1990, Alf's wife wandered into the kitchen and muttered that their neighbours had spare tickets for a Paul McCartney show in Birmingham.

"Oh I don't know, Jean. It would be a bit weird. I don't think so," he said.

But as the date approached, constant persuasion from Jean and the neighbours made Alf relent.

On the day of the show, Monday January 8, 1990, Alf and his friends Jeff and Anna Jones arrived at the city's NEC around 5PM.

On Anna's insistence, they made their way to the stage door.

About five minutes later, a giant limousine, surrounded by security, swept into view and headed straight into the arena. The giant metal doors of the venue closed imposingly after it.

"At this point, Anna leapt into action; she ran forward shouting, 'Alf's here! Alf's here!'. I'd been standing there wondering who was behind the wheel on the limo, you know, who was chauffeuring Paul around these days, doing my old job.

"The next moment a side door opened, and a security man came out and walked up to Anna, who was still shouting out that I was there."

The guard forced a smile and asked: "Can I be of assistance, lady?"

Anna replied: "I wonder if you could give my friend's card to Paul's PA. He's, erm, an old friend of Paul's."

With a withering look, which seemed to say, "yeah, that's original", the security guard went backstage to the dressing room.

"Two minutes later another official came to see us and said someone would be with us shortly. Then a third member of staff arrived and beckoned, 'Alf, will you please come with me?'

"My heart was in my mouth. What would I say? Would Paul recognise me with my long flowing beard? I clasped Anna's hand tightly."

Nervously he went backstage with Anna in tow.

He was soon in the VIP lounge, which was carefully decked out like a summer garden.

Alf and Anna clearly looked out place in the midst of group of elegantly-dressed theatre-goers, sipping champagne and clearly miffed at these new figures, who had dared to encroach on their ligging territory.

"We both picked up a glass of wine. My hand was shaking as I sipped.

"Then I heard a familiar sound booming out from about 30 or 40 feet away."

The voice called out: "Where is he?"

Clutching a cheese roll in one hand and a mug of tea in the other, Macca strolled into the room. Alf began to walk towards him and the singer's face beamed as he recognised his now very hirsute former employee.

McCartney brushed through the throng and grabbed Alf.

"Everybody around us seemed to stand still."

The pair hugged and Paul looked askance at Alf's new hairy look.

"Oh man, that beard's got to go," he laughed.

Alf recalls: "He asked me if Anna was my wife and I explained that she wasn't, but her husband was outside. Immediately he instructed security to have Jeff brought through.

"We chatted a bit more about the terrible deaths of Mal and John, and reminisced about the old days."

The bemused onlookers watched as the pair had a natter about all things Fab.

Then it was time for Paul to soundcheck but he insisted Alf, Jeff and Anna come through for a listen.

"The security guys put these VIP stickers on us and lead us out into this giant arena. There we were just the three of us, about seven rows back stretched out in this venue that is meant to hold up to 14,000.

"Before he started, Paul introduced me to his band. 'This is Alf. He was our driver back in the Sixties'.

"As he played, he would occasionally give me the thumbs-up. I tried to hold back the old waterworks and wondered if he would tease me like the old days if I got over-emotional.

"After an hour of wonderful music, Beatles songs and Paul's solo stuff, I was taken backstage again, where Paul introduced me to Linda."

That night, Alf, Jean, Anna and Jeff returned for the actual show.

Again, Alf was whisked backstage, so photos could be taken of him with Paul.

He made his way back to his seat as the lights dimmed and he settled down to watch his second McCartney performance of the day.

"Paul played 'The Long And Winding Road' and dedicated it to me. I just sat there, not applauding or anything, and looked around me.

"I looked at the faces, the smiling faces of the audience – so many happy people.

"It may sound schmaltzy, perhaps it was the sentiment of the song Paul was playing, but I remember thinking, *Wouldn't it be wonderful if the whole world was like this – happy and safe?*

"I said to myself, 'Thank you, Paul. God bless you. God bless The Beatles.'"